The Everyday Catholic's Guide to the Liturgy of the Hours

Daria Sockey

franciscan
media
Cincinnati, Ohio

LIBRARY OF CONGRESS CATALOGING-IN-PUBLICATION DATA
Sockey, Daria.
The everyday Catholic's guide to The liturgy of the hours / Daria Sockey.
pages cm
ISBN 978-1-61636-528-8 (alk. paper)
1. Catholic Church. Liturgy of the hours. 2. Catholic Church—Liturgy.
3. Divine office. I. Title.
BX2000.S63 2013
264'.02015—dc23
2012049149

ISBN 978-1-61636-528-8

Published by Franciscan Media.
28 W. Liberty St.
Cincinnati, OH 45202
www.FranciscanMedia.org

To Father Gerard Steckler, S.J., who, during a 1979 summer program in Spain, herded a bunch of us students to the university chapel each night to pray Compline. My prayer life has never been the same.

To my husband, Bill, who gave me my first breviary...
and so much more.

Let me confess up front that when Daria Sockey and her wonderful publisher invited me to enjoy the privilege of penning a few words for this book you hold in your hands, I quickly thanked them but informed them that I was *far* from their best option for the task. While I always have the most sincere of intentions, far too many days my fervent attempts to pray the Liturgy of the Hours are sporadic at best.

But in reality, perhaps that's what makes me the perfect advocate for the work Daria has compiled. *The Everyday Catholic's Guide to the Liturgy of the Hours* is a gift to those of us with the desire, but perhaps not the perfect knowledge, of how to make a commitment to pray this unceasing and universal prayer of the whole people of God.

Lord, open my lips.

And my mouth will proclaim your praise.

Most days, my morning begins with the ringing of the alarm clock, the rubbing of my eyes, a glance at my "non-morning person" husband still slumbering next to me, and the sound of these words ringing in my ears, courtesy of my smartphone. I pray Morning Prayer nearly every morning with the assistance of modern technology—my iPhone and the amazing YouTube videos created by David Rollins and his Penitentis channel sponsored by the Confraternity of Penitents.

As I pray along with this beautiful resource, my mind often unites with a special "saint" in my life, my beloved childhood pastor, Monsignor

Michael Collins. It was this holy Irish priest, transplanted into my Southern California parish, who gave me my earliest introduction to the Divine Office. A dear family friend, he often traveled with us on family vacations and camping trips. My recurring memory of Fr. Collins was his steadfast devotion to his morning office. He gifted our family with many Masses celebrated on the road and also with an example of how to perfectly begin a day—in prayer, specifically with the Hours.

Imagine my joy when, as a young adult, I learned that Fr. Collins's prayer was mine, too, and that committing myself to the Liturgy of the Hours united me with so many around the globe. With the breviary, I didn't need to be a priest to pray as Fr. Collins had done! Now, thanks to the Hours, my morning prayer unfolds as my day dawns. Morning Prayer sets the tone for my vocation to motherhood and the work of sharing my faith with others through my website and writing—it is the perfect start to my day.

Like you, I have many days when my first conscious thought is, *Not today, Lord. I'm too busy.* It happens more times than I care to admit. But I find now that on the days when that excuse begins to bubble up within me, I recognize that there is truly no way my first moments could be better spent. As a frequent traveler, I've learned that Morning Prayer is a constant that not only sets a tone for my day and expresses my priorities, it also unites me with loved ones living around the world. When I wake up on the road—as I often seem to do these days—and commence my day with the Hours, I am spiritually home.

O God, come to my aid.

O Lord, make haste to help me.

Midday Prayer often feels like a luxury. A computer alarm on my laptop all too often catches me midsentence while blogging or in the midst of editing or replying to the endless chain of emails. *Already?* is often my first thought. *Where has the morning gone?* This Hour is often prayed at my desk with the aid of the Universalis website. I've pondered on occasion investing in a beautiful print Breviary. I am attracted by the tactile feel, the ribbons, the sense of timeless tradition. But in honesty, today's digital access to the Divine Office fits my busy, wired lifestyle. I've trained myself to find a good stopping place in my work, to silence my heart, and to close the other tabs in my browser in an effort to keep Midday Prayer from becoming simply another "to do" item on my list. Am I perfect at keeping this hour? No, but I will attest to the benefits of Midday Prayer in setting the right course for both my productivity and my state of mind as the day progresses.

May the all-powerful Lord grant us a restful night and a peaceful death. Amen.

Night prayer is a challenge for me. I pray this particular Hour with the aid of the lovely Divine Office app on my iPad. As I fight to keep my eyes open for prayer, the voice of Dane Falkner, founder of the company behind this incredible gift of technology, rings in my ears. A geek at heart, I love praying with this app, which marries the beauty of the Psalms with the capacity to comprehend in some small way the universality of my prayer with others in the Body of Christ. One feature of the Divine Office app is a small virtual globe that rotates as I pray. At the top of the earth the app displays the number of people now in simultaneous prayer with me. Tiny dots of light pinpoint the surface of the spinning earth, marking the places where the app is in use. I pray this hour pondering my friend Fr. Roderick in Europe, the priests I prayed the Hours with in Israel last year, my son Eric studying in college back East, my parents in Mississippi, and my fellow praying moms not only across our country but also around the world. As I examine my conscience and pray the canticle, I lift not only my own soul to God but also those of my husband, sons, and extended family members as I drift off to sleep.

If you've picked up this book and are pondering whether The Liturgy of the Hours is for you, I urge you to take this journey with Daria. In the pages of her book, you will discover the heart and soul of this path of prayer. If you doubt your ability to commit to what can feel like a daunting devotion, emulate my "baby steps" and begin slowly. If you are someone who already has a tremendous devotion to praying the Hours, it's likely that Daria's work will open your eyes to new facets of your favorite prayer and help you to effectively share it with your loved ones.

In the Liturgy of the Hours, we have the amazing, and even unspeakable, privilege of meeting Jesus Christ in prayer and the privilege of uniting ourselves more fully with one another as Christians and also with the Liturgical Calendar of the Church. If you are already gifted with a devotion to the Hours, consider yourself blessed. For those of you about to embark on this amazing path of prayer, please know that now—perhaps more than ever before in your spiritual life— you are never alone. May God richly bless your efforts to better know, serve, and love him.

Lisa M. Hendey

To anyone who lives in friendship with God, it is natural to praise, to thank, to repent, to petition, and yes, even to tell him of our grief and our sufferings. Anyone who prays on a regular basis does these things. But praying with the Liturgy of the Hours takes these types of prayer to a higher level. To put it plainly, next to the holy sacrifice of the Mass itself, there is no greater way to pray than this.

> Then he told them a parable about the necessity for them to pray always without becoming weary. (Luke 18:1)

> Through him [then] let us continually offer God a sacrifice of praise, that is, the fruit of lips that confess his name. (Hebrews 13:15)

The Liturgy of the Hours is the Church's response to the command to "pray always." Its purpose is to sanctify time, to consecrate the phases of our day. The General Instruction on the Liturgy of the Hours puts it this way:

> By ancient Christian tradition, what distinguishes the Liturgy of the Hours from other liturgical services is that it consecrates to God the whole cycle of the day and the night.

> The purpose of the Liturgy of the Hours is to sanctify the day and the whole range of human activity.[1]

The opportunity to sanctify time is something we should welcome. Certainly we all value our time. We are always complaining that we do not have enough of it. We are disappointed with ourselves when we realize we've been wasting it. We marvel at the swiftness of its passing. We cling to our day planners and calendars as to anchors in a storm. So it makes sense to dedicate this valuable commodity—the fleeting hours of morning, noon, evening, and night—to our Creator. To give our work, our play, our rest, and our sleep to the one who understands their purpose and destiny better than we do.

In some sense, you may already be doing a little of that. If you make a daily morning offering or prayerfully commit yourself to God's protection before you go to sleep, you are engaging in a tradition that itself came from the older tradition of liturgical Morning and Night Prayer. By beginning the Liturgy of the Hours, you will be more closely connecting yourself to this ancient tradition.

Are you ready to begin the adventure?

PART ONE

Maybe this idea of "praying without ceasing" is a novel one for you. Maybe the thought of offering God every moment of your day is overwhelming. But maybe you're also feeling the call to do *exactly that*—and you just don't know where to begin. That's what Part I of this book is all about.

These first three chapters might be called "Liturgy of the Hours 101." Consider this section your warm-up: It will explain what the Liturgy of the Hours is, where it came from, why you should consider praying it, and what "equipment" you might need to be off and running. My heartfelt hope is that it will answer your basic questions—and leave your heart and mind hungering for more.

CHAPTER ONE

So, What Exactly Is This?

The Divine Office. Liturgy of the Hours. Matins. Lauds. Vespers. Evening Prayer. Breviary. You may have come across these words from time to time and wonder what they mean. You gather that they have something to do with prayers said at certain times of day—mainly by religious and clerics. These words might conjure up images of monks chanting in the cloister or a solitary priest reading from a chunky prayer book with ribbon markers.

Or maybe you know a little more than just the words. You may actually know *people* who pray from that chunky book. You're wondering if maybe you should try it yourself. But this seems like something of a project, and you're not sure where to begin. What are these prayers? Where did they come from? Why might I want to use these prayers, and how would I get started if I did?

What Is It?

The Liturgy of the Hours is "part two" of the official, public worship of the Catholic Church ("part one" being the Mass). As such, it is in a category of prayer different from private devotions, such as the rosary, novenas, litanies, chaplets, and even your own personal conversations with God. The word *liturgy* comes from the Greek *leitourgia*, which means "a public duty or service." Although a priest can say Mass by himself in the rectory, he isn't engaging in private prayer when he does so. He is still offering the Eucharistic sacrifice in the name of, and on behalf of, the entire Church. Something similar is going on with the Liturgy of the Hours. Those who pray it offer a "sacrifice of praise" in the name of, and on behalf of, the Church universal, whether they do so in a group or alone.

The Liturgy of the Hours—or Divine Office—consists of a repeating cycle of psalms, biblical canticles, Scripture readings, intercessions, hymns, and other prayers. These are arranged in seven daily sets, or "hours," each to be prayed during a specific phase in the day: morning, mid-morning, midday, mid-afternoon, evening, and night, plus one "floating hour" that may be prayed at any time. Like the Mass, some of its elements change with the seasons and feasts of the Church calendar. The book containing the Liturgy of the Hours is called the *breviary*.

Good to Know—"Hours? Seven of Them?"

Don't let the term *hours* scare you. This word refers to how the prayers mark and sanctify the various times, or hours, of the day. The typical liturgical hour takes maybe ten minutes to recite—longer, of course, if you do it with a group, chant it, or just take your time meditating on the prayers.

Seven breaks for prayer each day, even short ones, may sound like a bit too much for most of us. It is mainly in monasteries that all seven liturgical Hours are prayed daily. Parish priests typically pray five of them each day. Most laymen pray fewer still, focusing on one, two, or three of them. The most popular breviary for lay use only contains Morning, Evening, and Night prayer.

Who Is It for?

But isn't the Liturgy of the Hours mostly meant for monks, nuns, and clergy? No, no, and no! While only clergy and religious have a strict obligation to pray all or part of the Hours each day, laity are not only *permitted* to use this prayer, but are positively *encouraged* to do so. In reality, the most recent revision of the breviary in 1971 was done largely in order to make it easier for the laity to use, though that fact wasn't very well publicized. This is starting to change, thanks in particular to the Internet—and, I hope, resources such as this book.

> ### Good to Know—Papal Plea
>
> The last few popes have all urged lay Catholics to give the Liturgy of the Hours a try. Pope Benedict XVI said in 2011: "I would like to renew my call to everyone to pray the Psalms, to become accustomed to the Liturgy of the Hours, Lauds, Vespers, and Compline."[2]

As part of the Church's public worship, the Liturgy of the Hours is ideally prayed in group settings. Those in monasteries, convents, and seminaries can do this easily. Those in active religious communities might pray Morning and Evening Prayer in community but pray the other Hours in whatever location they carry out their work. Members of secular or "third" orders will pray one or more of the Hours together at their monthly meetings. In some parishes, Evening Prayer is offered on Sunday evenings—or Morning Prayer after early weekday Masses. Outside of these times, parish priests, deacons, and laymen mostly pray the liturgical Hours privately. The key point is, whether prayed alone, or with a group, the Liturgy of the Hours is the public prayer of the Church.

Where Did It Come From?

Next time someone tells you how much they admire Muslims for pausing five times a day to pray, tell them that Christianity had this custom long before there was such a thing as Islam. In fact, the liturgical Hours, in embryonic form, predated Christianity. Mosaic law prescribes prayer three times daily: morning, afternoon, and evening.

Psalm 55 says: "Evening, morning, and afternoon do I pray and cry, and he will hear my voice." The book of Daniel refers to that prophet's thrice-daily prayer, facing Jerusalem, during the Babylonian exile (see verse 6:11). These daily prayers were taken from the Scriptures. For example, the most important Jewish prayer, the *Shema*, comes from Deuteronomy 6:4–5:

Hear, O Israel! The LORD is our God, the LORD alone! Therefore, you shall love the LORD, your God, with your whole heart, and with your whole being, and with your whole strength.

The *Shema* is prayed twice daily. (This same passage appears in the Liturgy of the Hours every Saturday night.) Psalms and other Scripture passages make up these daily times of prayer. Besides the three principal times of prayer, it seems that the more devout would pray more frequently. Psalm 119 says, "Seven times a day I praise you" (verse 164). In the Acts of the Apostles, we see that the apostles and the first Christians—who were Jews—continued this practice of fixed-hour prayer in the temple, synagogue, and at home. There are references to these prayer times in Acts 3:1; 10:9; and 10:30.

Once the Gospels and letters of the apostles were written and circulated, these, too, were integrated into the early Christian liturgies. As Christian communities sprang up all over the Roman Empire and apart from the influence of Judaism, the custom of fixed-hour prayer changed in some places and faded away (at least as a universal practice) in others. But it was kept alive and cultivated by the desert hermits and the early monastic movement. Holy men and women, living consecrated lives of prayer, either solitary or in communities, recognized that the Psalms were the perfect prayer of God's holy word. Although the most zealous recited all 150 psalms each day, it was soon seen as more practical to pray them over the course of a week.

St. Benedict, the great sixth-century reformer and organizer of monastic living, came up with the form of the Liturgy of the Hours that has had the greatest influence on the way we pray it today. He was the one to name it the "Divine Office" and gave the hours their Latin names of Prime, Lauds, Terce, Sext, None, Vespers, Compline, and Matins. You will notice that this is not the biblical "seven times a day," but eight. Benedict's system specified prayer for every three hours around the clock. (The 3 A.M. hour of Prime was removed from the liturgy after the Second Vatican Council, so today we are back to a maximum of seven.)

The position and role of monastic and diocesan clergy evolved as the Church grew, and so did the liturgies they used. As cathedrals or monasteries were the anchors of society in the early Middle Ages, the bells that called priests and monks to prayer also drew in the laity from village and field. They would gather to listen as Lauds or Vespers were chanted. According to historians, the Divine Office *was* the daily liturgy most available during the week, for daily Mass, offered in public by parish priests, was not a universal custom at that time.

Eventually, however, lay participation in the liturgical hours dwindled. Some theorize that the rise of popular devotions in the vernacular, such as the rosary, were responsible. Indeed, the rosary—with its 150 Hail Marys taking the place of the 150 Psalms—could be seen as a devotional psalter substitute for those who could not read. Others say that when daily Mass in parish churches became widespread, the faithful gravitated toward it as their preferred daily liturgical prayer.

A long, dull article would be required to describe the differences among the many eastern and western religious orders in their practice of the liturgical Hours. Add to that descriptions of the many revisions, additions, and subtractions made to the Hours by the popes over the course of the Church's history and you'd have another full book! These pages will simply provide a few highlights.

Until this point, the psalms were chanted or recited either from memory or by directing one's gaze towards giant-sized books propped up at one end of the choir. (You can still see these oversized choir books in museums.) There was a psalter, lectionary, antiphonary, and hymnal. Given the amount of labor involved to produce a single, hand-copied volume, it's not surprising that each monk was not issued his own psalter. This arrangement worked, since monks seldom left their monasteries.

However, for a new and rapidly growing order, the Franciscans, this system became a problem. These traveling preachers needed a way to pray the liturgical Hours on the road—a way that did not require carrying a library of oversized volumes with them. There already was a small, hand-held book of Hours in use at the papal court, called the *Breviarum Curiae*, or breviary. (Note the Latin root that gives us the word *abbreviate*.) The Franciscans obtained permission to use this, substituting the Gallican (French) Psalter for the Roman one. As the friars wandered through Europe doing the Lord's work, their small, portable breviaries were noticed, and desired, by clergy and monks everywhere. Other major orders soon followed suit with breviaries of their own.

Several more centuries would pass before the invention of the printing press made these small, handy books available to any literate Catholic who wanted to pray the liturgical Hours. By then, many shorter "offices" were available, as well. These consisted of selected psalms and readings, grouped into fewer daily Hours. They were a way for laity and some active religious orders to pray the psalms according to a less intensive program. One example, which is still in use today, is the Little Office of the Blessed Virgin Mary.

Fast-forwarding to modern times, we see that the Divine Office has undergone many revisions over the centuries since the first breviaries of the Middle Ages. It was revised several times in the early twentieth century by Pope St. Pius X and by Pope Pius XII. But by far the most sweeping and dramatic revision of that century came as a result of the Second Vatican Council. The council fathers had several purposes in mind with this revision, among them:

- To simplify the Divine Office in order that it might become "the prayer of the whole people of God," with options enabling people to adapt its celebration to their state in life. This simplification included allowing the Hours to be celebrated liturgically in vernacular languages—and praying the psalms over the course of a month, rather than a week.

- To shorten the duration of the Hours so that it would be easier to pray them at the proper hours of the day and to order the psalms such that those which referred to the morning were prayed in the morning, those which referred to evening were prayed in the evening, etc.

- To add more variety to the canticles and readings and to add aids to understanding the meaning of the psalms.

- To make sure that the readings harmonized more closely with the cycle of readings at Mass and to create a better balance between the celebration of saints' days and the observance of the liturgical seasons.[3]

It was the Second Vatican Council reform that emphasized the name "Liturgy of the Hours" over the older "Divine Office." The purpose of the newer name was to emphasize what this liturgy was meant to do: to sanctify the hours of the day. But both names are still in use today.

Why Is This Still a Hidden Treasure?

It has taken quite a while for even a small minority of modern lay Catholics—other than third-order members—to notice the Liturgy of the Hours. Its use among the laity grew very slowly during the 1970s, 1980s, and 1990s, despite the fact that recent popes had certainly encouraged it. Starting in 2003, Blessed John Paul II devoted his weekly audiences to meditations on the psalms of Morning and Evening Prayer. This series was cut short by his death in 2005. Pope Benedict picked up where John Paul left off, halfway through the psalms of Evening Prayer, completing it in 2006. These talks are now available in book form (see resources chapter). However, efforts by bishops on the national and diocesan levels to promote the Liturgy of the Hours have been spotty, while only a limited number of pastors have introduced the Liturgy of the Hours, perhaps following daily Mass, or in conjunction with Eucharistic adoration.

Sparse pastoral action is not the only reason the Liturgy of the Hours is not better known. With two thousand pages of small print—and instructions that are confusing and even incomplete—the breviary itself has presented obstacles to Catholics who want to use it. Until recently, unless its new owner was willing to go to a parish priest for lessons, the breviary—purchased with enthusiasm from a religious bookstore—often ended up gathering dust on a shelf.

But progress continues to be made—and new computer technology is helping to clear the path for the laity. The liturgical Hours are now available as text and audio files on several online breviary websites, and mobile applications for phones and tablets make it possible for us to pray the Hours away from a computer. These sites and applications are soaring in popularity: Universalis.org reports one hundred thousand users per month, while Divineoffice.org reports forty thousand users daily—and has twice won reader-driven competitions for best website and mobile application. An international effort known as iBreviary.com also offers its mobile applications in many languages. And there is no substitute for personal witness: Catholic bloggers who pray the Liturgy of the Hours are posting with enthusiasm about the insights they have gained from this prayer, increasing awareness and interest among their readers.

This is where you have joined the party. Everything you need to pray the Liturgy of the Hours is at your fingertips. But *why* should you want to take the next step?

Words, Words, Words!

Liturgical prayer is beautiful, but complex. It has its own vocabulary. Think of the Mass and its many terms: Penitential Rite, Confiteor, Kyrie, Gloria, Creed, Offertory, Eucharistic Prayer, Consecration. Some we even know by both English and Latin names: Agnus Dei/Lamb of God. Yet these terms are second nature to any adult who attends Mass regularly and pays attention.

Similarly, the Liturgy of the Hours has a vocabulary of its own that can be confusing to newcomers—especially since there are often two different words for the same thing, one in English, and one based on Latin. So before we go any further, let's look at a brief list of the most common terms and their meanings.

Liturgy of the Hours/Divine Office—The public prayer of the Church, constituting, along with the Mass, the Church's liturgy. A repeating cycle of psalms, biblical readings, and other prayers, coordinated to the liturgical seasons, and feasts of the Church. The word *office* comes from a Latin word meaning *service* or *ceremony*.

Breviary—The book in which one finds the Liturgy of the Hours. The United States version is titled "Christian Prayer." The UK version is titled "Divine Office."

Morning Prayer/Lauds—One of the two principle Hours or "hinges" of the liturgical day, which may be prayed any time from when you wake up until mid-morning.

Evening Prayer/Vespers—The other principle Hour of the liturgical day, Evening Prayer is customarily prayed between 4 and 7 PM.

Night Prayer/Compline—To be prayed later than Evening Prayer, usually close to bedtime.

Daytime Prayer—A shorter liturgical Hour with three subdivisions:

Mid-morning/Terce; Midday/Sext; Mid-afternoon/None—The Latin names come from the Roman numbering of the hours of the day: Terce/third Hour (9 AM); Sext/sixth Hour (12 noon); None/ninth Hour (3 PM) Most laity and parish clergy pray only one Hour of Daytime prayer. Contemplative monks and nuns are more likely to do all three.

Office of Readings/Matins—Traditionally the hour which monks rose to pray at midnight, it now may be prayed at any time of day. The longest of the liturgical Hours, it consists of three psalms and two long readings, one from the Bible, the other from the fathers, doctors, and saints of the Church.

Psalter—Repeating, four-week cycle of psalms, canticles, prayers, and readings, this is the foundation of the Liturgy of the Hours. It is found in the middle section of the breviary.

Canticle—Poetic passage of the Old or New Testament that resembles a psalm and is recited or sung in the same manner as the Psalms.

Gospel Canticles—there are three of these:

Magnificat—Latin for the Canticle of Our Lady, recited during Evening Prayer.

Benedictus—Latin for the Canticle of Zechariah, recited during Morning Prayer.

Nunc Dimittis—Latin for the Canticle of Simeon, recited during Night Prayer.

Antiphon—A short verse that introduces and concludes each psalm and canticle, similar to the response for the responsorial psalm at Mass.

Proper of Seasons—The first third of the breviary, containing readings, antiphons, intercessions, and other prayers that replace parts of the four-week psalter during the holy seasons of Advent, Christmas, Lent, and Easter. The Proper of Seasons also contains special elements for each Sunday of the year.

Proper of Saints—A section in the last third of the breviary, giving the dates and prayers for saints' feasts and memorials.

Commons—A section of generic offices for celebrating a feast of Our Lady or of a saint, with headings such as common of pastors, common of holy women, common of martyrs, etc.

This should be enough vocabulary to satisfy the beginner. Don't worry—it isn't necessary to know all of these terms by heart in order to begin praying the Liturgy of the Hours. Just come back to this list as a handy reference when you need it. We will explore all of these terms in depth later on.

In the interest of simplicity, this book will stick mostly to the vernacular terms rather than the Latin—e.g., "Morning Prayer" rather than "Lauds." But please note that a passing familiarity with the Latin terms is helpful, since they are still in use all over the world, in Church documents, and in breviaries that originate in the U.K. and Europe.

CHAPTER TWO

Why Pray the Liturgy of the Hours?

There is no greater way to pray—outside of the Mass—than the Liturgy of the Hours. Yes, I know that's a bold claim. As I write this, I can almost hear the sputtering from coast to coast: "But, but, but, wait! What about the rosary? The Divine Mercy Chaplet? Meditation? And isn't it best if I just talk to God like a child talks to his father?"

Relax. To say that one kind of prayer is greater than others is not the same as saying, "You must ditch all of your other prayers and only focus on this one from now on." The Catholic Church is known for the wide variety of aids it offers us in our journey toward holiness and heaven. That some of these aids are intrinsically superior to others says nothing about whether God wants *you* to employ any of them beyond what is required by the precepts of the Church.

To use an analogy, think about vocations. The Church teaches that the priesthood and consecrated life are more perfect callings than the vocation to marriage. That doesn't mean that God wants all of us to be priests or religious. Quite the contrary. Similarly, your own "prayer vocation" may or may not include daily Mass or Liturgy of the Hours however excellent these are compared to other forms of prayer. It may or may not include the daily rosary, novenas to various saints, practicing the "Little Way" of St. Therese, the Divine Mercy Chaplet, litanies, *Lectio Divina,* daily Bible reading, Ignatian meditation, etc. No one can do everything—but everyone should do *something*. You prayerfully discern that something by taking into account the teaching of the Church, the unique circumstances of your own life, your own personal likes or dislikes, and the advice of a spiritual director, if you have one.

But, what makes the Liturgy of the Hours so special? This prayer transcends other prayers because:

1. It unites us to the Church universal.
2. It is liturgical.
3. It is scriptural.
4. It flows from and into the Mass.
5. It is the very prayer of Jesus himself.

Let's spend some time with each of those reasons.

1. Join the Throng From the Comfort of Your Home

It's 7:30 AM. After the flurry of activity required to get the kids out the door on time, they are, miraculously, on the school bus. I exhale gratefully and pour a cup of coffee. Sinking into my favorite chair, I reach for my breviary. It's time to join in the symphony of prayer that is rising to heaven from nuns in their cloisters, the pope in the Vatican, missionaries in far-off lands, priests, bishops, and laypeople all over the world. Rising from cathedrals, cinder-block mission chapels, city apartments, seminaries, mass transit vehicles, and homes like mine.

Lord, open my lips, and my mouth will proclaim your praise!

This symphony—a melody of praise, sometimes sung, sometimes spoken—travels from time zone to time zone, twenty-four hours a day, 365 days a year. It is like a flaming torch of prayer being passed around the globe, relay style, by spiritual athletes. This is what attracts so many people to the Liturgy of the Hours: the idea that, when we pray these daily psalms and readings, we are praying in union with our fellow believers around the world.

For example, each Sunday we catalog the wonders of creation, urging every creature to join us in praise of their Creator:

> Praise him, sun and moon,
> praise him, shining stars
> …
> sea creatures and all oceans,
> stormy winds that obey his word
> …
> beasts wild and tame,
> reptiles and birds on the wing. (Psalm 148)

Every Friday, we repent of our sins together with the most beautiful act of contrition ever written:

> Against you, you alone have I sinned;
> what is evil in your sight I have done
> …
> From my sins turn away your face,
> and blot out all my guilt
> …
> A pure heart create for me, O God,
> put a steadfast spirit within me
> …
> my sacrifice, a contrite spirit.
> A humbled, contrite heart you will not spurn. (Psalm 51)

Every evening, those who pray Vespers are united in spirit as they pray the identical Intercessions, bringing to the throne of God the needs of the pope, bishops, and priests as they carry out their ministry; of the sick, poor, and persecuted; of souls who have died that day.

Although it is possible to pray in our own words, or with favorite devotions, there is something powerful and satisfying about using the same words and forms used by millions of believers on each particular morning, midday, and evening. Praying the Liturgy of the Hours brings home the meaning of that phrase in the Creed, "I believe in the communion of saints." We, the faithful on earth, the saints in training, are joined in a unique way as we pray the psalms and canticles appointed to each day.

2. Liturgy for the Masses—Outside of Mass

As mentioned in the first chapter, the Liturgy of the Hours is, well, *liturgy*, distinguishing it from private devotions such as the rosary, novenas, and personal prayer. It is—along with the Mass—the official public worship of the Church. When we pray the Liturgy of the Hours, we are exercising the common priesthood of the faithful, which we possess in virtue of the sacrament of baptism.[4]

By delegating to the laity the ability to pray the Liturgy of the Hours, not just as a private devotion, but as "an action of the Church,"[5] the Church has granted us an enormous privilege. Think of it this way: Suppose you were too ill to attend Mass on a Sunday, but instead read the Mass of the day from a missal. Though a very worthwhile action, it is only an act of devotion, not an act of liturgy. You would not have "offered Mass," for only a priest can do that.

Now think about the Liturgy of the Hours. Although the Church tells us that the ideal way to pray the Hours is to do so in a group with a priest or a religious presiding, this is not required in order to make the Hours a liturgical action. As long as you are using an approved Office, your recitation of the Hours, even when alone at home, is a liturgical action, joined to that of the Church universal:

> In this public prayer of the Church, the faithful (clergy, religious, and laypeople) exercise the royal priesthood of the baptized. Celebrated in "the form approved" by the Church, the Liturgy of the Hours is truly the voice of the Bride herself addressed to her Bridegroom. It is the very prayer which Christ himself, together with his Body, addresses to the Father.
>
> The Liturgy of the Hours is intended to become the prayer of the whole People of God. In it Christ himself "continues his priestly work through his Church." His members participate according to their own place in the Church and the circumstances of their lives: priests devoted to the pastoral ministry, because they are called to remain diligent in prayer and the service of the word; religious, by the charism of their consecrated lives; all the faithful as much as possible.... The laity, too, are encouraged to recite the Divine Office, either with the priests, or among themselves, or even individually.[6]

In the past, there was a distinction made between praying the Divine Office liturgically (what priests and maybe religious did) and praying it devotionally (what the laity did). Since Vatican II, all the documents indicate that laity have now also been delegated to offer the Hours as liturgy. Unlike clergy and religious, we are not obligated to do so. We are merely given the opportunity.

And it's an opportunity too good to miss.

3. Praying the Word

Over the last few decades, Catholics have made tremendous strides in reading Sacred Scripture in addition to what is already read *to* them at Mass. They've advanced from not reading the Bible much at all, to knowing they *ought* to be reading it more, to actually reading it!

So here's another benefit to making the Liturgy of the Hours a part of your day. It combines prayer and Scripture reading all in one. Even if you only say Morning and Evening Prayer, you'll become extremely familiar with about eighty psalms, several dozen Old and New Testament canticles, and fifty-some short readings from the epistles. Should you tackle the Office of Readings, with its daily page-long passages of Scripture, you'll be going over significant parts of many Old Testament books, arranged to map out the plan of salvation as the Church moves through the liturgical year.

But here's the really exciting part: With the Liturgy of the Hours, you are not just *reading* the Bible, but also *praying* it. That is, you are using the word of God to praise, thank, and petition him. Hallowed tradition refers to the Our Father as the Lord's Prayer. That's because Jesus gave us these words in answer to the request of his followers to teach them to pray. Yet the psalms, all divinely inspired, are also truly the Lord's prayers! They, too, will teach you how to pray: how to praise, how to thank, how to repent, how to petition, and even how to complain to God about suffering and injustice. It just makes sense to pray in the words that God gave us.

This is not to denigrate spontaneous or self-composed prayers. Yes, our Father loves to hear us speak to him in "our own words," just as parents delight in the stumbling speech of their toddlers. But aren't we also thrilled when our children mature and learn to express their thoughts with increasing clarity and intelligence? By praying the psalms each day, we gradually absorb their language and attitude. In a 2011 general audience, Pope Benedict explained this concept:

The Psalms are given to the believer exactly as the text of prayers whose sole purpose is to become the prayer of the person who assimilates them and addresses them to God. Since they are a word of God, anyone who prays the Psalms speaks to God using the very words that God has given to us, addresses him with the words that he himself has given us. So it is that in praying the Psalms we learn to pray. They are a school of prayer. Something similar happens when a child begins to speak, namely, he learns how to express his own feelings, emotions, and needs with words that do not belong to him innately but that he learns from his parents and from those who surround him... and little by little he makes them his own, the words received from his parents become his words and through these words he also learns a way of thinking and feeling, he gains access to a whole world of concepts.... This is what happens with the prayer of the Psalms. They are given to us so that we may learn to address God, to communicate with him, to speak to him of ourselves with his words, to find a language for the encounter with God.[7]

4. Living the Mass

The Eucharistic sacrifice, as the Catechism tells us, is "the source and summit" of the Christian life (*CCC*, 1324). Sunday Mass should be the spiritual highlight of our week; daily Mass—if we are fortunate enough to be able to get there—the highlight of our days. All the rest of our prayer should flow into and out of the Mass. There is no better way to make that happen than—you guessed it—the Liturgy of the Hours. In fact, it has been said that the Mass is a precious jewel, and the Liturgy of the Hours is the golden setting.

It's easy to see why. The Liturgy of the Hours follows the Church calendar, observing its seasons, solemnities, and feasts. There are antiphons, readings, and prayers particular to those seasons and days. So our daily experience of the Hours provides both a fixed daily pattern for prayer, yet with enough variety to prevent boredom. Praying the Hours keeps us aware of whatever the Church is commemorating or celebrating each day throughout the year. It helps us to remain mindful of the holy seasons of Advent, Lent and Easter, no matter what distractions our jobs or family responsibilities bring to our days. It extends and amplifies each Mass we attend with psalms, antiphons, and readings that complement it perfectly.

Take, for example, a holy day such as the Solemnity of the Assumption on August 15. Sure, we make it to Mass sometime between the evening of the fourteenth and the evening of the fifteenth. But imagine bringing the meaning of this great feast back to our minds and hearts once, twice, or three times more throughout that day? The Liturgy of the Hours is tailor-made for this sort of holy day mindfulness. On the vigil, for example, the psalms are bracketed by these antiphons:

> Christ ascended into heaven and prepared an everlasting place for his immaculate Mother, alleluia.

> Through Eve the gates of heaven were closed to all mankind; through the Virgin Mother they were opened wide again, alleluia.

The Office of Readings contains an excerpt from Pius XII's Apostolic Constitution on the Assumption of the Blessed Virgin Mary, giving us a quick tour of the importance of this doctrine and its support by various fathers and doctors of the Church through the ages. Morning Prayer for the Assumption makes the heart leap with this beautiful antiphon:

The daughter of Jerusalem is lovely and beautiful as she ascends to heaven like the rising sun at daybreak.

Evening Prayer concludes the feast with a short reading that reminds us that the Assumption has significance for each of us personally (see 1 Corinthians 15:22–23) and this concluding prayer:

All powerful and ever living God, you raised up the sinless Virgin Mary, mother of your Son, body and soul to the glory of heaven. May we see heaven as our final goal and come to share her glory.

One more example. Take an ordinary weekday during Advent. This is the time of year when our frantic preparations for Christmas (ironically) often make it difficult for many of us to enter into the spirit of joyful expectation and longing that the season demands. When we do find a few minutes to sit still and pray, we are too tired to think—or our minds are racing towards the next item on our Christmas to-do list. To pray well on our own steam would be impossible. But flip open the breviary or pull it up on your iPhone, and for a few blessed minutes you can leave the holly-jolly behind with no trouble at all.

You're immersed in Isaiah, joining the people of Israel, as they walk in darkness and long for the light of the Messiah. You're listening to the voice of prophecy—and are given the words to beseech the Savior to come without delay. If you use the Office of Readings, you'll get a new meditation on the Incarnation from the Church Fathers every day. Evening Prayer? There are short readings from the Apostles about the second coming of Jesus, for this, too, is an event we should train ourselves to long for during Advent. From December 17 onward come the splendid "O" antiphons of Evening Prayer, each naming Christ with one of his prophetic titles. Yes, we may be pulled in ten different directions during December. Praying the liturgical Hours will pull us in the *right* one.

In chapter seven, we will come back to the liturgical year. The point here is simply this: If you are not able to attend daily Mass, the Liturgy of the Hours is the next best thing. If you do attend Mass, the Liturgy of the Hours will keep you immersed in its beauty and power all day long.

5. Christ Is Here

Talk show host David Letterman originated the humorous Top Ten List, starting with number ten and counting down, all the while becoming progressively more witty. His aim was for number one to be the funniest one of all. In my list of the Top Reasons to Pray the Liturgy of the Hours, it would be difficult to put most of the reasons in some kind of order or importance. Except for number one—the *top* reason to pray the Liturgy of the Hours:

> *In the psalms of the Liturgy of the Hours, you will meet Jesus.*
> *You will pray with him and in him. Jesus will pray with you and in you.*

This is where it all comes together: Christ is present in the Liturgy of the Hours *because* this prayer is scriptural, liturgical, and united to the Mass. But what are our indicators that Christ truly is here?

Messianic Meanings

We find signs and hints of the Savior throughout the psalms. Jesus himself referred to the messianic prophecies of the Psalms: "Everything written about me in the law of Moses and in the prophets and the psalms must be fulfilled" (Luke 24:44). Psalms is the Old Testament book quoted most often to support the claims of the Gospel. The New Testament writers state that in the life and actions of Jesus, many prophecies in the Psalms were fulfilled. For example:

"Not a bone of his shall be broken." (Psalm 34:20)

"The stone that the builders rejected
has become the cornerstone." (Psalm 118:22)

"I will open my mouth in parables." (Psalm 78:2)

"Zeal for thy house consumes me." (Psalm 69:910)

These are only a few. Jesus applies several passages from the Psalms to himself. Perhaps the best known of these is Psalm 22, which begins, "My God, My God, why hast thou forsaken me?" These profound and terrible words, uttered from the cross, illustrate the depth of Jesus's physical, mental, and spiritual anguish. But that is not all. By summoning the strength to utter aloud the opening verse of Psalm 22, Jesus was inviting us to see that the entire psalm was being fulfilled in his passion, death, *and* his resurrection. Psalm 22 has been called the "fifth gospel" because it can so easily be interpreted as applying to the Lord's sufferings—as well as his triumph.

Praying the Psalms daily, you will gradually become adept at noticing symbols or "types" that point to Jesus. Many references to a king, for example, can be applied to Jesus, the son of David. Psalms describing the "just man," who sometimes suffers at the hands of evildoers but in the end is vindicated by God, can also be prayed with Jesus in mind, since he is the sinless man, the only one to whom the word *just* applies completely.

The Prayers He Prayed

Another way to see Christ in the Psalms is to visualize him praying them. The Psalms were the prayers and hymns of Israel, prayed at morning, noon, and evening by faithful Jews. Jesus learned them at his mother's knee, perhaps repeated them with Joseph during a midday break from work, and studied them in the synagogue. Our spirits will be enriched if, as we pray the Hours, we sometimes meditate on the Psalms in the Ignatian style: by picturing Jesus praying them in various scenes from the Gospels.

Imagine him as a young man worshiping in the synagogue, repeating the prophetic, messianic psalms, aware that he was about to fulfill them! Imagine him praying them in his sufferings. St. Jerome says that Psalm 56 tells of the Lord's passion, and St. Augustine says this of Psalm 57. The Church places Psalm 88 on his lips for the liturgy of Good Friday. Since Jesus quoted from both Psalm 22 and Psalm 31 ("Into thy hands I commend my spirit") while on the cross, it is appropriate to imagine him praying these other psalms of dread and pain in Gethsemane.

He Prays Them Still

Best of all, Our Lord's praying of the Psalms isn't just something that happened two thousand years ago. We already know that in the Mass, Christ eternally offers his one sacrifice for our redemption. Those moments of atonement ("Father, forgive them") and surrender ("Into thy hands") on Calvary reverberate through history and into eternity through the Eucharistic sacrifice as offered by our priests. In a similar way, Jesus offers an eternal sacrifice of praise to his Father that is made present here on earth when *we* offer the Liturgy of the Hours.

Don't just take my word that this is so. The General Instruction on the Liturgy of the Hours says quite explicitly that "it is the very prayer that Christ himself, together with his body, addresses to the Father."[8]

St. Augustine spoke eloquently on this prayerful union:

"Our Lord Jesus Christ, the Son of God, who both prays for us, and prays in us, and is prayed to by us. He prays for us, as our Priest; He prays in us, as our Head; He is prayed to by us, as our God. Let us therefore recognize in him our words, and his words in us."[9]

Read the above quote several times, and realize what a profound union with Jesus we have when praying the Liturgy of the Hours. It would be hard to find a clearer and more moving argument for joining in the sacrifice of praise.

Good to Know — Top Reasons to Pray the Liturgy of the Hours

1. You get both daily Scripture reading *and* prayer done at the same time.

2. It takes less than ten minutes each for the hours of Morning, Evening, and Night Prayer if you're reading it by yourself. (An "hour" never went by so quickly!)

3. If you can't get to daily Mass, it's the best substitute.

4. By praying the Divine Office, you are joining in the universal prayer of the Church being offered by your brothers and sisters in Christ all over the world.

5. You will be praying the exact same prayers that Pope Benedict prays each day.

6. You will be participating in a tradition that is nearly as old as the Church itself.

7. It is a painless way to memorize lots of Scripture.

8. You will have a pattern for daily prayer that gives you the ease of a familiar routine, but with enough daily variation to prevent boredom.

9. You will acquire an impressive vocabulary that includes words like *breviary, vespers, Te Deum, compline,* and *antiphon!*

---

10. You will be praying "with the same words used by Jesus, present for millennia in the prayer of Israel and of the Church" (Bl. John Paul II).

11. You will be fulfilling the wish of Pope Benedict that all Catholics become familiar with the Liturgy of the Hours.

12. You will be performing a liturgical act that does not require the presence of a priest, instead exercising the priesthood of the laity and joining your praise to that which Jesus, the great High Priest, offers to His Father.

Just Do It

Of all the chapters in this book, this one was the most difficult to write. I recognize that it is here that readers will either be intrigued enough to go on—or will close the book, concluding that the Liturgy of the Hours is no more special than their usual prayers.

In conclusion, I turn to John Brook, a convert from New Zealand. His words resonate with me—and speak so clearly to the power of the Divine Office:

> Without the Office, our prayers can follow the same old track, saying the same things over and over again, boxed into our own small world. The Office explodes that box and opens us to experience the whole Church praying the mind of Christ, praying for the world for which he suffered and died.
>
> The Divine Office provides a pattern of prayer which helps to solve the most common difficulties in prayer. It is a way of praying rooted in the Scriptures, in the experience of Jesus, and in the life of his Church. It is a way that has been proved by countless Christians from the earliest times.[10]

CHAPTER THREE

Breviaries and Other Resources

To conclude Part I, I'd like to highlight the many outstanding resources that are blessings for those who choose to travel this road.

If this book had been written twenty years ago, this would be a pretty slim chapter. At that time, there was the complete, four-volume Liturgy of the Hours and the one-volume edition for Morning, Evening, and Night Prayer. A couple of shorter books containing limited selections of the liturgy rounded out the inventory of resources. That was it.

But thanks to the Internet revolution—and, even more recently, the increasingly widespread use of various mobile devices—the Liturgy of the Hours is available in many formats, at little or no cost to anyone who is wired (or wire*less*). There is online "how-to" information on praying the Hours, plus forums and blogs where fans of the Hours can ask questions and share insights. There are several devotional commentaries on the Psalms for those who wish to deepen their understanding of scriptural prayer.

Everything is now in place to fulfill the Church's desire for the Liturgy of the Hours to become "the prayer of the whole people of God." Everything, that is, except more people who know about it and have a desire to pray it.

Digital or Hard Copy: Pros and Cons

Deciding which breviary to use (or what mixture of the two) may seem like a no-brainer to some. For those who spend much of their life online, digital breviaries are an obvious choice. In a similar vein, passionate members of the "hate-staring-at-screens-love-holding-a-real-book" party will have already made their decision, as well. For the undecided, here are the potential merits and drawbacks of each.

A Book in the Hand

Pros

• A print breviary is traditional. If you are going to join a parish or monastic group for prayer, you will want to learn to use one.

• A print breviary is far better for reference. If for some reason you want to look up a reading from several days ago, or look ahead at what's coming up, it's faster and easier with the book.

• A print breviary is a sacramental. It has a certain permanence and significance that a website or app does not have.

• For many, using a book is more conducive to a prayerful, contemplative spirit.

• You aren't dependent on the availability of a cell or wireless signal in order to pray.

• You can purchase a yearly guide that tells you which pages to use each day of the year.

Cons

• The instructions in the printed breviary are not user-friendly, not complete, and thus frustrating to many.

• A breviary is heavy and inconvenient to carry when traveling. It does not fit easily in a woman's purse. It's all too easy to forget to bring it along.

• A breviary isn't cheap, especially if you want the complete, four-volume edition containing all the liturgical Hours.

Going Digital

Pros

• Easy, easy, easy—no flipping around from psalter to propers to commons! Everything is laid out each day for you. Digital is the obvious choice for a beginner or someone who has tried and failed with a print breviary. It removes any guesswork and gets you praying immediately.

• Portability: If you already carry a smart phone, an iPod, or a Kindle, you'll never leave home without the day's prayers. Women won't suffer from Heavy Handbag Backache Syndrome.

• There's even a digital breviary that has audio files of each day's prayer—a big help for aural learners, those with dyslexia or poor eyesight, commuting drivers, and others.

• If you already have a computer, online breviaries are free. Mobile apps are free or low in cost compared to a print breviary.

Cons

• Backlit screens have a different effect on our eyes and brains from the printed page. Praying the Hours from a screen may not feel comfortable or prayerful to everyone.

• Power outage? Out of luck. Ditto for traveling in remote locations.

Personally, I use both hard copy *and* digital breviaries. All of the reasons listed above influence me in one situation or another. This is the case with most people who come to love praying the Liturgy of the Hours: they mix it up.

Now for a closer look at some of the products out there. Keep in mind that prices are only approximate.

Print Breviaries

Liturgy of the Hours, **4-volumes,** by Catholic Book Publishing Company. The complete breviary in use in the United States, it is also used in many other English-speaking countries. It's the breviary used by your pastor. It contains all seven liturgical Hours, arranged by volume to follow the liturgical year. Two volumes cover the thirty-four weeks of Ordinary Time, one covers Advent through Christmastide, and one covers Lent through Pentecost. There are regular- and large-print editions; there are leather- or vinyl-covered editions. Starting at $120, this is clearly an investment. It is, of course, possible to buy each volume separately as you need them over the course of a year, making for a softer initial impact on your bank account.

Christian Prayer: The Liturgy of the Hours by Catholic Book Publishing Company. This is the most popular breviary for laypeople. This single-volume breviary focuses on the hours the Church most recommends: Morning, Evening, and Night Prayer. There are also selections from Daytime Prayer and the Office of Readings. Personally, I have never found these "selections" useful. Part of the attraction of the Liturgy of the Hours is saying prayers specific to each day in union with the Church universal. Using these selections would put you out of sync with the rest of the Church. But they do give you a little taste of Daytime and Office of Readings—perhaps whetting your appetite to go on to embrace the full breviary. Price: around $38, making for a more economical foray into liturgical prayer.

The Mundelein Psalter edited by Douglas Martis and Samuel Weber. Ideally, the Liturgy of the Hours should be sung in whole or part. In monasteries it is still chanted, either in Latin or English. This is fairly difficult for much of the laity to tackle. Although the breviaries listed above have a section of Psalm tones (repeating melodic lines that fit the psalms and canticles), the psalters in these breviaries are not "pointed," or marked with asterisks and italicized words to let one know where the voice should change from one note to another. To the rescue comes the *Mundelein Psalter*. It is a one-volume breviary containing Morning, Evening, and Night Prayer. Each psalm or canticle is headed with a simple melodic line, and the text is marked so that you know where to change notes. In addition, the hymns in the *Mundelein Psalter* are the official texts from the *Liturgia Horarum*, given both in Latin and in English. These hymns are of more ancient origin than most of those appearing in other American breviaries, and they are therefore a delight to the tradition-minded. There's even a technical support site with MP3 files of the chants for anyone who has trouble reading the music. If the idea of singing the psalms attracts you, this is the one-volume breviary for you. Note, however, that the *Mundelein Psalter* is larger and heavier than other one-volume breviaries—a consideration for anyone with arthritic hands. Price: $50.

Catholic Book Publishing Company also offers a self-contained volume of the complete **Daytime Prayer** ($12). This book would be an inexpensive way to supplement the one-volume **Christian Prayer,** giving you four liturgical hours for the year in their entirety. The only thing lacking would then be the Office of Readings (described in detail in chapters four and six), which could then be accessed via the Internet.

Abbreviated Print Breviaries

Shorter Christian Prayer by Catholic Book Publishing Company. This breviary contains the complete four-week psalter for Morning and Evening Prayer. It does not contain all of the propers (variations) needed for the liturgical seasons or for most saints' feasts. This slender volume is less intimidating to the newcomer, but for the same reasons mentioned above about the "selections" in the one-volume breviary, this would not be the right book for someone who wants to follow the correct sequence for the entire liturgical year. Price: $16.

Evening Prayerbook-Sunday Vespers by Sacros Press. The Holy Father, in his letter *Dies Domini,* asked that Catholics find ways to extend their keeping of the Lord's Day beyond Sunday Mass. To this end, the Second Vatican Council had suggested the restoration of Sunday Vespers (Evening Prayer) in parish churches or in the home. The *Evening Prayerbook* ($29) contains just that—Sunday Vespers for the entire year, in a colorful, user-friendly format. Each Sunday's prayer appears on a large-type, two-page spread; no searching or flipping required. Sacros also publishes the *Night Prayerbook* in the same format ($23). Both of these are easy ways to introduce family members to the Liturgy of the Hours. To order, go to www.liturgyofthehours.org and click on the Gift Shop tab.

In the U.K. and British Commonwealth

The Divine Office by Harper Collins. This is the title of the British complete breviary, which fits everything into three volumes, rather than the American four. These are purchased separately at £32.50 each ($72.45 in Canada).

Daily Prayer by Harper Collins. This single-volume breviary for the region contains the complete Morning, Daytime, Evening, and Night Prayer, and so is more comprehensive than the American one-volume version (£32.50; $78.75 in Canada).

Morning and Evening Prayer by Harper Collins. This volume includes what the title says, plus Night Prayer (£23.95; $47.84 in Canada).

Note also that all Harper Collins breviaries use Scripture readings from the Jerusalem Bible rather than the New American Bible.

Good to Know—Just a Little Taste

There are books and subscription devotionals, some by Catholics and some by other Christians, that present daily scriptural prayer in forms similar to that of the Liturgy of the Hours. The popular *Magnificat* magazine, for example, includes morning and evening psalms and Gospel canticles with antiphons. Thanks to *Magnificat*, thousands have acquired a taste for praying the Psalms, and have "graduated" to the Liturgy of the Hours. But to clarify, the psalms in this periodical are not the complete, designated Morning and Evening Prayer of each day.

Episcopalian author Phyllis Tickle has a popular series of books called *The Divine Hours*. It is based on the Anglican *Book of Common Prayer* (itself a non-Catholic version of the Divine Office, composed when the Church of England broke away from the Catholic Church). Books such as this are not bad books: Nothing is wrong with reading selections of Scripture arranged over the calendar year. But they are not liturgical books approved and prescribed by the Catholic Church for praying the Liturgy of the Hours. If you want to pray the Catholic liturgy and receive the full benefits described in the previous chapter, then be sure to use an approved Catholic breviary. Somewhere in the first few pages, look for "approved for use" or "approved by" the bishops of your country.

Digital Breviaries

iBreviary. Founded by Fr. Paolo Padrini, this Italian-based website offers the Liturgy of the Hours online in many languages. iBreviary also has the first mobile application of any kind to receive Vatican approval. The online version interfaces well with Amazon Kindle, making a mobile breviary of sorts available to those who do not have a smart phone or a tablet computer. The free mobile application is available for most phones and tablets, including Kindle Fire; more than 200,000 people worldwide use it. *ibreviary* also contains a daily missal and many other prayers and Church rituals, thus coming in handy for traveling clergy—or anyone who finds themselves frequently away from home.

Divineoffice.org. Arguably the most popular digital breviary in the United States, Divineoffice.org has won numerous Reader's Choice Awards for best Catholic website and mobile app. No subscription is needed if you are using the Internet. The mobile application costs $20. A special feature of this breviary is its audio component. Each of the hours is available not only in written form, but as a podcast, so that you can listen to the hours as you pray. This tool is invaluable to those who want to learn how the prayers of the Liturgy are said in community. It's also great for commuters, who may listen as they drive to and from work, and perhaps for busy mothers, who might overcome a time crunch by listening to Evening Prayer as they fix dinner.

Universalis.com. Based in England, Universalis is another popular digital breviary that you can use online for free. The free version avoids copyright expenses by offering its own translation of the Psalms and the Jerusalem Bible for all other Scripture. The paid versions for PC and mobile devices also offer the Grail Psalms/New American Bible to match American print breviaries. You will also find the free version of Universalis embedded in the *Laudate* Catholic prayer app. Purchase of the Universalis app ($21; £15 in the UK) gives you access to the entire, full-year Liturgy of the Hours. This means you can pray it with a mobile device even when no Wi-Fi or cell signal is available.

Ebreviary.com. This site offers each liturgical hour of the day up to a month in advance, in PDF format. Free to read online, a $49.95 yearly subscription enables you to legally print as many booklets of any hours needed for a group recitation. This is a good service for small groups in a parish or other organization that prays the Hours together on an occasional basis, but not often enough to justify the expense of buying breviaries for everyone.

How-To Resources for Beginners

Theoretically, your breviary should tell you everything you need to know about how to pray the Liturgy of the Hours. For example, currently the one-volume Christian Prayer has "General Principles" from pages 34 to 37, plus the "Ordinary" on pages 686–698. These two sections taken together really do tell you most of what you need to know, except for rubrics (i.e., when to make the Sign of the Cross, or when to bow, stand, or sit when praying with a group).

But judging from the questions asked on my website—and scores of remarks from "Divine Office Drop-Outs"—this has not worked out very well in practice. There are still sixteen pages of fine print to slog through and apply to the various sections of the breviary. These instructions seem to assume a certain grasp of liturgical vocabulary—and that the newcomer is probably learning to pray the Office from the example of others. An unassisted layperson must be very motivated to figure all of this out, and it's no surprise that some give up. Fortunately, there are resources to help you.

St. Joseph Guide for the Liturgy of the Hours by Catholic Book Publishing Company. This inexpensive annual booklet tells you which page is needed in the psalter, propers, and/or commons for every single day of the year. Editions are available for both the four-volume and one-volume editions: Check to make sure you order the one you need. A new guide must be purchased each year ($3).

This book. Using the St. Joseph guide is very helpful. But it's also so important to understand the principles of the liturgical year and the contents of your breviary so that you can eventually figure out by yourself which pages you should be on. Chapter seven of this book will explain some of that, as well as some of the options for praying the various elements of the liturgical hours in accordance with the Church's instruction. (See chapters 5 and 6.)

Any online breviary. Even if you can't stand the idea of praying online, these handy websites are a great way to check your progress on learning to choose the correct prayers for each day.

Discovering Prayer by Seth Murray. Go to www.rosaryshop.com and click on the "General Info" tab, and then "Liturgy of the Hours." From there, follow instructions to download this free tutorial. If you benefit from it, the author would appreciate a donation or your shopping at his religious articles online store. Highly recommended.

Coffee & Canticles. This is my blog for fans of the Liturgy of the Hours. There's a How-to tab with "Divine Office Boot Camp": a series of posts that briefly explains how to pray the Hours. We also have a weekly Q&A post so that readers may ask any questions about the Liturgy of the Hours. Researching the relevant Church documents, I usually come up with the answer: www.dariasockey.blogspot.com.

Divine Office for Dodos by Madeleine Pecora Nugent (Catholic Book Publishing). If you've done the ***Discovering Prayer tutorial*** listed above and are still confused, you might benefit from the more detailed approach of ***Divine Office for Dodos.*** Its ninety-two chapters use an incremental, "baby steps" method. If you are a fast, intuitive learner, you might find "***Dodos***"a bit tedious. But if you want lessons, complete with review questions in the encouraging voice of your favorite grade-school teacher, this is the book for you ($9).

The St. Thomas More House of Prayer. At this lay-run retreat house in Northwestern Pennsylvania, all the liturgical Hours are prayed each day by a community of local volunteers. Their mission is to teach newcomers how to pray the Liturgy of the Hours. If your travels take you to this part of the country, a detour off Interstate 80 to learn the breviary in a gorgeous woodland setting would be well worth it. Overnight accommodations are available. For more information, go to www.liturgyofthehours.org.

For Deeper Understanding

Once you know the mechanics of praying the Liturgy of the Hours, you will be able to focus on how to pray the psalms with the mind of the Church. Chapter eight of this book should help a bit. If you want more, try some of the following commentaries and meditations.

The School of Prayer by John Brook. This small, chunky, information-dense volume on the what, why, and how of the Liturgy of the Hours includes the author's commentary on the entire psalter of Morning and Evening Prayer. These comments manage to bring in elements of biblical history, theology, and devotions. A how-to section references the UK Harper Collins breviary. Highly recommended ($27).

Psalms and Canticles: Meditations and Catechesis on the Psalms and *Canticles of Morning Prayer* by Bl. John Paul II. The late and beloved John Paul II pursued the aim of Paul VI to encourage the laity to pray the Liturgy of the Hours. Over the course of several years, he devoted each Wednesday audience to a different psalm or canticle of Morning and Evening Prayer. The Morning Prayer talks have been published as a collection by Liturgy Training Publications ($25). You may find the Evening Prayer commentaries (continued by Pope Benedict after John Paul's death) on the Vatican website.

Reflections on the Psalms by C.S. Lewis. Everyone's favorite non-

Catholic, yet nearly Catholic, author explores various facets of the psalms (such as praise, death, cursing, judgment, and nature) in twelve essays ($9).

Praying the Psalms by Thomas Merton. A lengthy essay (forty-five pages) in which this modern spiritual master explains why the Church considers the Psalms the most perfect book of prayer. Merton celebrates the variety found in the Psalms and how praying them enables us to surrender ourselves joyfully to God's will. Highly recommended ($7).

Singing in the Reign by Michael Barber. Don't let the silly title fool you. This book is an in-depth Bible study on the book of Psalms, explaining how the Psalms, as ordered in the Bible, form a unified whole that tells the story of God's covenant with David. The book also goes deep into the christological meaning of the Psalms, as well ($10).

The Revised Grail Psalms by Benedictine Monks of Conception Abbey (GIA Publications). Our breviaries currently use the Grail translation of the Psalms, which was developed in England in the early 1960s when the liturgy began changing towards the vernacular. Its purpose was to create an English psalter that would work well with Gregorian chant. The Revised Grail Psalms, done by American Benedictines, is said to be a more accurate translation that still retains chant-ability. The Revised Grail Psalms will be the translation used in the upcoming new edition of the American breviary. (It is already the approved psalter in Kenya.) This event is three to five years down the road, but if you are interested in a glimpse of the future today, the Revised Grail psalms are available in a standalone volume for personal study ($12). This book you are reading also uses, with permission, passages from the New Grail Psalms—hence the slight variation you will find between psalm excerpts that appear in this book and those in your breviary.

PART TWO

So you made it through Part I and want more! The next step—and the goal of Part II—is to look more closely at the structure and elements of the Liturgy of the Hours.

I'd like to make an important note here, however. If, after reading chapters 1 through 3, you are so excited about the Hours that you just can't wait to start praying, then feel free to take a pause here in this book and dive into your breviary to get going. Come back to these chapters when you feel the need for clarification.

On the other hand, some people are more detail-oriented. They want lots of information before moving forward. Before buying a product, they read dozens of consumer reviews. Before going on a trip, they map out the route and line up every hotel and attraction. Detail-oriented people read instruction manuals, and then, like the tortoise in the fable, pass up the intuitive hare who used the wrong size screw in step 12, and now has to go back, take things apart, and start over. If you are a details person, then enjoy the next few chapters, which will show you not only the forest, but also the trees of the Liturgy of the Hours.

CHAPTER FOUR

"Seven Times a Day I Praise You": The Liturgical Hours at a Glance

Think of this chapter as an outline, or a schematic, or a zoomed-out map of the entire Liturgy of the Hours. Its purpose is to show you the big picture. Most laymen, at least in the beginning, only pray one or two of the liturgical Hours each day. But it's good to see where those one or two Hours fit into the entire liturgy.

As stated earlier, there are seven liturgical Hours in all, which mark and consecrate to God the various hours of the day. Each layman needs to discern which one(s) work with the rhythm of his or her life. Here they are in order.

Morning Prayer

Also known as Lauds (from the Latin word for "praise"), Morning Prayer is the first hour of the day, unless it is *not* the first Hour of the day (see Office of Readings). As its name suggests, it is said at the beginning of the day. In a monastery, that might be at the crack of dawn. For the rest of us, somewhere between 6 and 9 AM would make sense. Morning Prayer consists of:

1. Opening verse: "God, come to my assistance, Lord, make haste to help me." This is said while making the Sign of the Cross and is followed by the Glory Be.

2. A hymn, generally considered optional, especially for those praying alone.

3. Psalmody: Two psalms and one canticle, each beginning with its own antiphon, concluding with the Glory Be, and the antiphon repeated. (The repeat of the antiphon is optional but a very widespread custom.) In American breviaries, the two psalms are also followed by optional psalm prayers.

4. A short reading, usually from the New Testament.

5. A responsory to the reading.

6. The morning Gospel canticle, known as the *Benedictus* or Canticle of Zechariah. Like the psalms, it is preceded by an antiphon, then followed by the Glory Be, and the antiphon repeated.

7. Morning Intercessions.

8. The Our Father.

9. The concluding prayer.

10. The closing blessing: May the Lord bless us, protect us from all evil, and bring us to everlasting life. Amen (said while making the Sign of the Cross).

Daytime Prayer x3

There are three Hours of Daytime Prayer: mid-morning (terce), midday (sext), and mid-afternoon (none). The Latin names come from the ancient numbering of the Hours of the day, which was considered to begin at 6:00 AM, making 9:00 the third Hour, 12:00 (noon) the sixth, and 3:00 the ninth Hour. They are also referred to as the "little Hours" due to their brevity. All three daytime Hours are generally observed in monasteries, where the liturgical Hours are primary to the vocation of the religious who live there. For active religious, parish priests, and laity, the Church suggests that one daytime Hour is chosen: whichever of the three corresponds most closely to the time chosen for prayer. Mid-morning prayer would occur between 9:00 and 11:00 AM; midday prayer around noon or just before or after your lunch hour; and midafternoon prayer later still, up until 3:30 or 4:00 PM.

The format for each daytime Hour is as follows:

1. Opening verse: God, come to my assistance. Lord, make haste to help me. This is said while making the Sign of the Cross, and followed up with the Glory Be.
2. Hymn (optional).
3. Psalmody: Three psalms *or* three sections of a longer psalm, with antiphons and Glory Be, as described above for Morning Prayer. Note: On Sundays and feasts there is only one antiphon for the entire psalmody of Daytime Prayer, which is prayed once before the first psalm, and repeated at the end of the third.
4. A very short reading from either the Old or the New Testaments.
5. A two-line responsory verse.
6. Concluding Prayer.
7. Concluding acclamation: Let us bless the Lord / And give him thanks (while making the Sign of the Cross).

Evening Prayer

Evening Prayer, or Vespers, marks and sanctifies the completion of the working day. In a monastery, where the day begins early and ends early, it might be said as early as 3:30 PM. Those of us who live in the world might do it at the conclusion of our day job, or link it to dinnertime (just before or after). It follows a pattern identical to Morning Prayer (see above). The one difference is that the evening Gospel canticle is the Canticle of Mary, better known as the Magnificat.

Night Prayer

Night prayer is associated with the completion of one's day. It is said close to bedtime. Even if you go to sleep in the small hours of the morning, Night Prayer is appropriate for you. Night Prayer is short, and it runs on a simple, seven-day repeating cycle, making it a great Hour for beginners to pray as they learn the rhythms and rules of liturgical prayer. Here is its format:

1. Opening verse: O God, Come to my assistance, etc.
2. A brief examination of conscience, followed by an act of contrition.
3. Optional hymn.
4. Either one psalm with antiphon and the Glory Be or, on Saturday and Wednesday, two very short psalms with antiphons and the Glory Be.
5. Short reading.
6. Responsory.
7. Gospel Canticle: the Canticle of Simeon, also known by its Latin title, *Nunc Dimittis*. It is preceded by an antiphon, concluded with the Glory Be, and the antiphon is repeated.
8. Concluding Prayer.
9. Concluding blessing: May the all-powerful Lord grant us a restful night and a peaceful death. Amen.
10. A Marian antiphon, for example, the Hail Holy Queen, the Hail Mary, or one of several others listed in your breviary. Recite or sing, Latin or English.

Good to Know—Adapt! Adapt! Adapt!

In its instructions on the Liturgy of the Hours, the Church urges us laity to adapt our recitation of the Hours to our situation. That certainly applies to the timing of the Hours mentioned above. If you are a late sleeper, for example, there is nothing wrong with praying Morning Prayer at 10:00 or 11:00 AM, or even noon, if that is when your day begins. Someone who works night shifts might find it fitting to pray Evening and Night Prayer at 7:00 and 10:00 AM in the morning, since for them, these hours signal—respectively—the end of the workday and bedtime.

Suppose I just happen to forget about my breviary until noon? Do I start with Morning Prayer, or move right into Daytime Prayer? The answer is, whichever you prefer: stick with the principle Hours of the day (Morning and Evening) no matter what time it is, or keep up with the actual time of day. The choice is yours.

Office of Readings

The Office of Readings requires a greater commitment of time (fifteen to twenty minutes) and attention (the two long readings require a more concentrated, intellectual focus than do the psalms). This is one reason that the Church says it may be done any time of the day, according to our particular needs and daily schedule. It may even be prayed on the preceding day, after Evening Prayer, by way of a vigil. Prior to Vatican II, this hour was called *Matins* (from the Latin word for morning) because it was said *very* early in the morning, before *Lauds* or Morning Prayer. Here is the format for the Office of Readings:

1. Opening verse: O God, come to my assistance, as in the other hours.
2. Hymn (optional).
3. Three psalms, or three sections of a longer psalm, with antiphons.
4. Reading I: a longer reading (500+ words) from the Bible, Old or New Testament. Generally, a particular book of the Bible is covered for one or two weeks at a time.

5. A short verse/response.

6. Reading II: a reading of similar length from one of the Church fathers, doctors, or saints. Occasionally there is a second reading from the documents of the Second Vatican Council. Sometimes the reading is a direct commentary on the previous biblical reading; other times it is on a topic related to the liturgical season, or about the day's feast.

7. The concluding prayer.

8. Closing acclamation, as in daytime prayer:

9. On Sundays and solemn feast days only, a prayer called the *Te Deum* is also recited just prior to the concluding prayer of the Office of Readings.

Did I Say Seven?

Although these are the seven Hours of the liturgical day, there is also a kind of eighth Hour that is optional for the eves of Sundays, solemnities, and feasts. It's called, fittingly, Vigils. You will recall the Easter Vigil Mass, with its many extra readings. The Office of Vigils has this same sort of feel to it. It consists of several canticles and a Gospel reading that are read immediately after the Office of Readings, but before the *Te Deum* on the eve of the Sunday or feast in question. In monastic communities of strict observance—such as the Carthusians—the office of Vigils is prayed in the middle of the night, with the monks actually rising from sleep to welcome the Sabbath, just as many Catholics welcome the feasts of Christmas and Easter with midnight Mass. Unless you regularly pray the Office of Readings on the evening previous to its Sunday or feast day, you probably won't be interested in Vigils. If you do want to pray Vigils, you will find that the easiest way to do it is to use an online breviary. Otherwise, you will find what you need for Vigils in an appendix to each volume of the four-volume breviary.

There you have it—the big picture of the Liturgical Hours. More detail of each Hour will come in chapter six. But first, let's zoom in and take a close look at each *element* of liturgical prayer—and the role each of them plays in the overall Liturgy.

CHAPTER FIVE

Taking It Piece by Piece

Psalms, antiphons, canticles, responsories, readings: The Liturgy of the Hours contains so many different items. Why are they there? What are they for? In this chapter, we'll see how each element fits into the whole and how each item of them helps us to pray well, both for ourselves and on behalf of the whole Church. Much of the information in this chapter comes from the "General Instruction of the Liturgy of the Hours"—a document that appears in full at the beginning of the four-volume breviary and can also be easily accessed online.

But First... the Invitatory: Preface to Your Liturgical Day

There is one element of the Liturgy of the Hours that has not yet been mentioned because it does not belong to any one of the Hours and because it is optional. But this particular option is almost universally used and loved by those who pray the Hours. The invitatory psalm is an opening or introduction to the entire day's sequence of prayer. It is used either before the Office of Readings or before Morning Prayer, depending on whichever one is prayed first in the morning. It does what its title suggests: invites us to praise God and to listen to him. We begin the invitatory sequence with this versicle (that is, short verse), said while tracing—with the thumb—the Sign of the Cross on our lips:

Lord, open my lips / and my mouth shall declare your praise.

Next, there is an antiphon, which varies each day. The invitatory antiphon is found in each day's psalter, either before the Office of Readings or before Morning Prayer. The default invitatory psalm is 95. Alternative choices for the invitatory are Psalms 100, 67, and 24. Here are the opening verses of each one:

> Come, let us ring out our joy to the Lord; hail the rock who saves us (Psalm 95).

> Cry out with joy to the Lord, all the earth. Serve the Lord with gladness (Psalm 100).

> O God, be gracious and bless us and let your face shed its light upon us (Psalm 67).

> The Lord's is the earth and its fullness, the world and those who dwell in it (Psalm 24).

All of these psalms remind us that God is both the mighty Lord of creation and the merciful Father who looks after our welfare. All include the invitation to praise him.

A beginner trying to become familiar with the breviary might find the invitatory psalm to be one step too many. In this case, it might be a good idea to skip it until the habit of Morning Prayer has become familiar and easy. But afterward, the invitatory is worth adding in. This is the single psalm that you will pray every day of the year, and thus you will have it by heart in no time. Once memorized, you may even wish to pray the invitatory as you rise from bed, long before you get around to opening your breviary.

On a personal note, my husband is such a big fan of the invitatory psalm that he thinks that even people who don't pray the Hours and have no interest in doing so ought to be encouraged to just learn Psalm 95—or one of its alternates—and use it as their daily prayer upon rising. I tend to agree with him. It's a fantastic way to start your day. When your first words of the day are, "Lord, open my lips," you are thereby acknowledging that language is God's gift, submitting your power of speech to him and asking that your communication fulfill its highest purpose: to "declare your praise." By tracing the Sign of the Cross on our lips, we also use the language of gesture to put our mouth under the direction of our Savior for the day.

Of course, the invitatory psalm is completed by its antiphons, which can't easily be memorized, since they change each day. It is suggested that the antiphon to the invitatory be repeated after each strophe (indented section of verses), just as we do with the responsorial psalm at Mass. Alternatively, it may simply be repeated at the beginning and end of the psalm, as usual, with other psalms in the Liturgy of the Hours.

One last note: If you pray the invitatory psalm, you proceed directly into the psalms of the Office of Readings or Morning Prayer without saying the Opening Verse.

Opening Verse

O God, come to my assistance
  Lord, make haste to help me.

Every liturgical Hour (except the one you preface with the invitatory psalm) starts with this verse from Psalm 70. For all our talk about the sheer praise of God being the highest form of prayer, we always begin our praises with this plea for help.

Why? Because we need it. We need help if we are to pray well and worthily, with attention to our prayers and a minimum of distraction.

And praying, as we are, on behalf of the whole Church, we are asking, with this verse, for divine assistance with all the needs of the body of Christ—so very, very many. For guidance for our pope, bishops, and priests; for more vocations; for all who suffer—the sheer magnitude of spiritual and temporal need in this world is staggering. No wonder we start out each hour like a drowning man: "*Help!*" However serenely we might chant or speak these words, that is what we are doing. The difference is that we know to whom we call out—and are confident that the Lord will answer our plea.

As we say these words, we make the Sign of the Cross. As in the invitatory, this combination of gesture and speech enables us to speak two languages at once. While calling for help, we proclaim faith in the only two things that matter: the Holy Trinity and the Redemption. Having begun our prayer with this plea that echoes back even to ancient Israel, we children of the new covenant are now ready for the task at hand.

The Glory Be

The Opening Verse is followed by the Glory Be, also known as the *doxology*. This word comes from Greek words that mean "speaking praise." The term refers to a short, liturgical hymn of praise. Other examples of doxologies include, "Through him, with him, and in him" at the end of the Eucharistic prayer at Mass, and "For the kingdom, the power, and the glory are yours" after the Our Father.

But the Glory Be is often referred to as *the* doxology. This very ancient profession of faith in the Trinity occurs as a frequent refrain in Catholic worship and prayer. It ends every decade of the rosary, for example. Many hymns have a version of it as the final verse. You will typically use this invocation five or six times whenever you open your breviary. Why so often? Well, the Trinity, as mentioned earlier, is the central reality from which everything else flows: creation, redemption, salvation, eternal life. We really cannot recall it too often. In addition, we follow up the prayer of Israel with the doxology in order to frame each psalm in the fullness of revelation that we have received with the coming of Jesus. You will notice that the version of the Glory Be that appears in your breviary—ending, *as it was in the beginning, is now, and will be forever, Amen*—is different from the one normally used during the rosary. This is the same Glory Be in both cases. The one in the breviary is simply a different version, which has left off the final Latin phrase, *et in saecula saeculorum* (translated as "world without end" in the traditional Glory Be). It is quite possible that this version could be replaced in the future with either a return to the traditional form or even a newer version, since the Latin phrase in question has several different meanings. In many other languages, it is translated *for ages upon ages*. If you prefer the traditional version of the Glory Be when you pray the Hours, feel free to use it.

> **Good to Know—A Gesture of Awe**
> There is a traditional rubric (liturgical gesture) for the Glory Be. One should bow the head, or bow slightly from the waist, while saying, *"Glory be to the Father and to the Son and to the Holy Spirit."* This helps us remember the profound awe in which we should hold the mystery of the Holy Trinity.

Hymns: To Sing or Not to Sing

One of the most frequent questions I get asked is, "Are the hymns required or optional?" After studying what the Church has to say about hymns in the "General Instruction for the Liturgy of the Hours," my usual response is, "Strongly recommended to the point of almost being required for a communal celebration, and optional but still urged for your consideration when praying alone."

The long explanation is that hymns are a particularly fitting way to praise God, and praise is what the Liturgy of the Hours is all about. Furthermore, singing is a traditional element of the Hours, stemming back to its earliest history. The literary beauty of many hymns can be a great aid to devotion—and can help draw us into the spirit of the various liturgical seasons. It's easy to see the sense of singing a hymn to open a liturgical Hour when praying with a group. We open Sunday Mass with song, don't we? Hymns help make us aware of the formal, liturgical character of the Hours.

On the other hand, we can extend the Mass analogy to what happens when we are praying alone, or with a very small group that doesn't feel musically adept. As widespread as hymns are on Sundays, they are equally scarce at weekday Masses. There are two main reasons for this. First, songs require both a leader and a large enough congregation to successfully carry off the hymn. These may not be available consistently during the week. Second, it is often desirable for weekday Masses to be brief to accommodate those whose daily schedules won't allow for extended worship.

This same situation applies to those who pray the Liturgy of the Hours alone or with a friend or two. If an extra minute or two makes or breaks your desire or ability to pray the Hours, this might be a good reason to skip the hymn altogether. If singing out loud by yourself feels less exalting than embarrassing, then you should pass. However, it doesn't hurt to read through the hymn as if it were a poem or perhaps sing it to yourself, inside your head, if you happen to know the melody. The choice is yours.

If you compare several breviaries (one-volume, four-volume, online, American vs. British), you will notice that the choice of hymn for the day is not standardized the way the psalms and readings are. Before the revision of Vatican II, there were official hymns to go with each day's liturgical Hours. These hymns—in Latin or their English translation—may still be used. Many of them still appear in the UK *Divine Office* and in some of the online breviaries. In the United States, they are available in the *Mundelein Psalter* (see chapter three).

The most widely used American breviaries have substituted other hymns, both traditional and contemporary, for many of the Roman breviary hymns. Although the General Instruction permitted the introduction of different and/or contemporary hymns, many believe that this permission was not meant to allow the wholesale substitution of new hymns for all of the ancient ones. It is thought by many that the Roman hymns have withstood the test of time in terms of their poetic quality and theological content. In their November 2012 decision to prepare a newly amended and retranslated text of the breviary, the United States bishop affirmed this opinion. The preliminary plan is for the Roman hymns to be translated into English and restored to a place of prominence in the Liturgy of the Hours, although the use of other hymns will still remain a legitimate option.

Antiphons

Every psalm and canticle has a pair of "bookends" known as antiphons. The word itself comes from Greek roots "anti" (prior to) and "phoneo" (sound or speech). So the antiphon is a short line said before the main "speech" of the psalm or canticle. The antiphon helps us to understand the psalm or canticle in a number of ways. In general, it gives us a theme or central thought to go with the psalm. The antiphon might highlight an idea that would not normally occur to us if we read the psalm without it. Best of all, the antiphon often brings out the christological meaning of the psalm, helping us see how it has been fulfilled by Jesus. We talked about these messianic meanings back in chapter two. The antiphon will often save us the guesswork, showing us right up front how to find Christ in the psalm.

Antiphons vary during liturgical seasons and on feasts. These changes help us to pray the psalm in the light of that particular day's Office. Take, for example, Psalm 42, which is a poem of longing for God, of overwhelming grief, and of hope. Here is some of it:

Like the deer that yearns
for running streams,
so my soul is yearning
for you, my God.
My soul is thirsting for God
the living God;
when can I enter and appear
before the face of God?
My tears have become my bread,
by day, by night,
as they say to me all the day long,
"Where is your God?"

...

Deep is calling on deep,
in the roar of your torrents;
your billows and all your waves
swept over me...
With a deadly wound in my bones,
my enemies revile me,
saying to me all the day long,

"Where is your God?"

...Why are you cast down, my soul;

why groan within me"

Hope in God; I will praise him yet again,

my saving presence and my God (Psalm 42).

Now, watch how the antiphons give us different ways to pray this psalm. During ordinary time, when we see this psalm on every fourth Tuesday morning, the antiphon is:

When will I come to the end of my pilgrimage and enter the presence of God?

The antiphon encourages us to focus on longing for heaven, both for ourselves and for the whole Church, as we journey through life and deal with inevitable suffering.

But when we pray this psalm on Tuesday of Holy Week, the antiphon is:

O Lord, defend my cause; rescue me from deceitful and impious men.

Clearly, this is the voice of Jesus, overwhelmed with grief in Gethsemane, anticipating the hatred and the mockery of his enemies—"He trusted in God; let him deliver him now, if he wants him" (Matthew 27:43). So on this day we pray Psalm 42 in his name, recalling his bitter passion.

When Psalm 42 pops up again during the Easter season, the antiphon once more has us longing for heaven, but with greater joy, focusing on the beautiful nature imagery of the first verse, leaving out the reference to life's weary pilgrimage, and instead recalling the living water of sanctifying grace:

As the deer longs for flowing streams, so my soul longs for you, my God, alleluia.

Psalm 42 is also used in the Office of the Dead, which is used on All Soul's Day and on other occasions when we wish to remember the faithful departed. Here, the antiphon is:

My soul is thirsting for the living God; when shall I see him face to face?

With this antiphon, we envision and voice both the longing and the hope of souls in purgatory.

Repeating the antiphon at the end of the psalm, after the Glory Be, is optional (good to know when you are in a hurry). But it's a very popular option. Repeating the antiphon helps you to refocus if your mind has wandered, and gives the psalm a sense of completion.

A Note on the Psalms

The psalms make up the greatest part of the Liturgy of the Hours. They are more than just another "element" of the Hours; they are the heart of it. No person reading this book is going to wonder why the psalms are in the Liturgy of the Hours the way they might wonder about antiphons or responsories. At the same time, there is so much to learn in order to appreciate the psalms properly—and to pray them on an ever-deeper level—that entire books could be (and are!) written about them. Chapter eight will explore some concepts that help us to pray the psalms with greater understanding.

Old and New Testament Canticles

Canticles appear in the psalmody of Morning and Evening Prayer, and they are prayed in the same manner as psalms: prefaced by an antiphon and concluded with the Glory Be and a repeat of the antiphon. The word *canticle* comes from the Latin *cantare*, to sing. Canticles are hymns, poems, or prayers from many different books of the Bible.

Each day at Morning Prayer there is a canticle from the Old Testament after the first psalm. There is a different Old Testament canticle for every weekday of the four-week psalter. On Sunday, the canticle is always a part of the "Song of the Three Children" from the book of Daniel, chapter three. This very long canticle is split into two parts. One of them is used on Sundays I and III; the other on Sundays II and IV. The canticles come from thirteen different Old Testament books, although nearly a third of them come from the book of Isaiah.

Evening Prayer has canticles from the New Testament, this time, following the two psalms rather than sandwiched in between. There aren't nearly as many canticles from the New Testament as from the Old: Only seven are repeated over the course of the week, plus one that is used only during Lent, and another one (see 1 Timothy 3:16) that is only used on the two "theophany" feasts of Epiphany and the Transfiguration. Four of the weekly New Testament canticles come from the book of Revelation, where they are clearly the hymns of the saints in heaven, sung before the Lamb of God. The others come from the letters of St. Paul. Some of these are thought to be early Christian hymns that St. Paul used to teach the truths of the faith in his letters.

New Testament canticles seem to be the culmination of the day's psalmody. Throughout the day, we have been praying in unity with our fathers in faith, the people of Israel, albeit with antiphons that show us the fulfillment of the old covenant in Jesus. Now, at the end of the day, that fulfillment is proclaimed explicitly as we proclaim our redemption with a hymn of the new covenant.

Psalm Prayers

Readers on my blog often ask about the psalm prayers: "Are the psalm prayers optional?" "When I go to a local monastery to join in Vespers, they never say the psalm prayers. Why is that?" And, from a reader in England, "What on earth are these psalm prayers you refer to?"

The purpose of the psalm prayers is to help us reflect on the meaning and application of the psalm. According to the General Instruction of the Liturgy of the Hours (GILH), these psalm prayers were to appear in a supplement to the breviary, since they were for optional use. What has happened in practice is that American breviaries have incorporated psalm prayers directly into the psalter (not a supplement or appendix), while the breviaries of most other countries don't have them at all, even as a supplement. Beginners, in particular, can find the psalm prayers useful in helping them understand the significance of a given psalm, since these prayers will often point out either the christological meaning of the psalm, or its application to the spiritual life.

However, those who have been praying the psalms for some time and have learned to see these meanings on their own might find the psalm prayers redundant. (This may be why visitors to seminaries and monasteries often do not hear the psalm prayers being used.) In this cases, it makes sense to forgo them. Those who have families and work schedules to attend to often skip the psalm prayers, as well, simply in the interest of saving time. The best thing to do is to try it both ways to see whether or not these prayers are helpful to you, and act accordingly.

Note: Since the official Latin breviary *(editio typica)* does not include the psalm prayers in the body of the psalter, the US bishops have decided to eliminate them from the proposed revision of the American breviary.

A Moment of Silence

This is a good place to take note of the "short silence" mentioned in the General Instruction. This is an often-overlooked element of the Liturgy of the Hours. Sections 201 through 203 of the General Instruction is devoted to this concept. A brief pause at the end of a psalm or reading is recommended in order to reflect on what has been read. The Church wisely suggests that this silence not be prolonged to the point where those participating become bored or annoyed.

Naturally, if you are praying by yourself, you may pause to reflect for as long or as short a time as you wish. The point of sacred silence is not to make a lengthy meditation that you may not have time for, but rather enough of a pause to turn you back from inevitable distractions and keep you mindful of what you are doing. It might take no more than one deep breath to accomplish this. Or, you might wish to devote half a minute or more to reviewing a psalm: finding again the verse that surprised you, moved you, or taught you something new.

Captions and Quotations

The red-ink captions and black-ink quotations beneath the title of each psalm are optional extras to help your understanding. The caption is a brief phrase describing the focus of the psalm, for example, "the Messiah's royal power"; "the lament of people in war and famine"; "the joyful song of those entering God's temple." This red-ink phrase is not to be said aloud; it is not part of the day's prayer. Rather, it is there to let you know what to expect in the psalm or canticle you are about to recite. Like the Scripture reference (chapter and verse) that is given in black, it's there for information purposes only, and you do not even have to read it to yourself if you don't care to do so.

The black-ink quote beneath the caption comes from either the New Testament or from the Fathers of the Church. This quotation makes a connection between the psalm or canticle and the message of the Gospel. For example, we recite the canticle of Hannah (1 Samuel 2:1–10) on Wednesday morning of Week II in the psalter. (This is the one where the long-barren Hannah rejoices in the answer to her prayers in the birth of the baby Samuel.) The quotation beneath the title is from Mary's canticle, the Magnificat: "He has cast down the mighty from their thrones and has lifted up the lowly. He has filled the hungry with good things" (Luke 1:52–53). The similarities between Mary's canticle and Hannah's are startling, and this short quote will put you in mind not only of the similarities in the two canticles, but also the differences and similarities of the two mothers.

The psalm for Wednesday morning of Week II, Psalm 97, has been commented upon by St. Athanasius: "This psalm foretells a world-wide salvation and that all nations will believe in Christ." That is a bold claim, but sure enough, these verses indicate that Athanasius was on to something.

> The Lord is king, let the earth rejoice;
> let the *many* islands be glad
>
> ...
>
> The skies proclaim his justice;
> *all peoples* see his glory (emphasis mine).

Since these verses are buried in a psalm about God's glory and power, the quotation in this instance helps us see something we might otherwise have missed. Normally, these quotations are not meant to be read as part of the Liturgy. However, the General Instruction states that they may be used in place of the regular antiphons during ordinary time when the office is recited, not sung.

To sum up, the psalm prayers, captions, and quotations are optional items that help us pray the psalms and canticles with understanding, in particular with understanding of their connection to the Gospel. It is up to you how much to make use of these. And don't forget the importance of brief silence now and then during your prayer. These are the moments when public worship and private devotion blend together.

Readings

The psalmody is done. You've been praising, thanking, repenting, and petitioning on behalf of the Church for some time. Now, it is time to sit back and listen as God says something to *you*. Most of the liturgical Hours—the Office of Readings is the one exception—have pretty short readings. During Daytime and Night Prayer, the reading might consist of a single verse of Scripture. If your mind is wandering, you might zip through the reading and hardly notice it at all.

According to the General Instruction, the readings are brief for a purpose. These short passages are often heard at Mass, but as part of a much longer reading. Isolating a key verse or two draws our attention to a message that we might not notice when it is "buried" in a longer reading. Here are a few examples of these short but sweet readings:

> Who will separate us from the love of Christ? Trial, or distress, or persecution, or hunger, or nakedness, or the sword? No, in all things we are more than conquerors because of him who has loved us. (Romans 8:35,37, Morning, Wednesday, Week II)

> Whatever you do, in word or in deed, do everything in the name of the Lord Jesus, giving thanks to God the Father through him. (Colossians 3:17, Midday, Sunday, Week IV)

> There is no condemnation for those who are in Christ Jesus. For the law of the Spirit of life in Christ Jesus has freed you from the law of sin and death. (Romans 8:1–2, Evening, Friday, Week IV)

Stay sober and alert. Your enemy the devil is prowling about
like a roaring lion, looking for someone to devour.
Resist him, strong in the faith. (1 Peter 5:8–9, Night Prayer,
Tuesday, Week ?)

The beauty of these short readings is that they are easy to understand,
give you something profound to think about, and stay with you. After
a few months or a year of praying the Liturgy of the Hours, these
readings will become old friends that will pop into your consciousness
at the times—temptation, discouragement, suffering—when you most
need them.

This being said, the General Instruction allows for substituting a
longer form of the reading or even an alternate reading (if desired and
if there is a good reason), during weekdays of ordinary time. The one-
volume *Christian Prayer* breviary gives somewhat longer versions of
some of the readings in Morning and Evening Prayer than those that
appear in the four-volume breviary. Perhaps this decision was made
to give some extra scriptural nourishment to those who use the one-
volume version, since they do not have the benefit of the Office of
Readings.

Responsory
As its name implies, this short verse or verses after the reading is meant
to be our response or acclamation to what God has told us in the
reading. The responsory is meant to turn us from reading to prayer and
contemplation.

There are two things for beginners to note about the correct way
to pray the responsory. You will see that it is split into parts, with
every other line marked with a red dash. This setup assumes a group
recitation, where either a leader plus the rest of the group, or the group

divided into two sections, takes turns saying every other line. If you are praying alone, it is permissible, and makes more sense, to not say the repeated opening line. Second, the responsory for Morning and Evening Prayer includes the *first half* of the Glory Be, but instead of the second half ("as it was in the beginning…"), one should instead follow up with the concluding line of the response.

Gospel Canticles

Morning, Evening, and Night Prayer each follow the reading and responsory with a Gospel Canticle, distinguished from the New Testament canticles discussed earlier by their being outside of the "psalmody" section—and because they are the only extended selections from the Gospel that appear on a daily basis in the Liturgy of the Hours. These are:

• The *Benedictus*, which is the canticle uttered by Zechariah upon the birth of John the Baptist. This canticle praises God for John's birth and announces his future as the forerunner of the coming Messiah. It is recited at Morning Prayer.

• The *Magnificat*, Mary's song of praise in response to Elizabeth's, "Who am I that the mother of my Lord should come to me?" This is the Gospel canticle of the evening.

• The *Nunc Dimittis*, or canticle of Simeon, who told God he was now ready to die because he had lived to see the infant Savior, "a light of revelation to the nations, and the glory of your people Israel." It is recited at Night Prayer.

The Gospel canticles are placed near the end of their respective Hours as a way of honoring them. This is because there is an order of precedence in all the psalms and canticles: Old Testament first, then New Testament; among New Testament passages, non-Gospel first, then Gospel. You will notice this same order during the Liturgy of the Word at Mass. The three Gospel canticles also come in their chronological order in the Bible over the course of the day.

When you pray the Liturgy of the Hours in a group, it is appropriate to stand during the Gospel canticle, just as we stand in respect for the Gospel at Mass.

The antiphons for the *Benedictus* and the *Magnificat* were chosen carefully to coordinate with the liturgical year. Even during ordinary time, each Sunday has specific antiphons that come from the Gospel of the day's Mass. Weekdays of liturgical seasons also have special antiphons for these canticles. Those of the last seven days of Advent are particularly well known. They are called the "O" antiphons, each one beginning with "O" and giving a prophetic name for the Messiah. We also know these antiphons as the verses to the hymn, "O Come, O Come Emmanuel."

Intercessions—and How *Not* to Say Them

Morning and Evening Prayer both contain intercessions that follow the Gospel canticle. These are similar in form to the Prayer of the Faithful at Mass. Although the primary purpose of the Liturgy of the Hours is to offer to God a "sacrifice of praise," the Church notes in its instructions that the Jewish/Christian traditions of prayer have never sharply separated praise and petition. Indeed, the psalms themselves often jump around from praise to thanksgiving to repentance to petition and back again in a way that may seem dizzying until one gets used to it! It is natural, in fact, for petition to flow from praise. We've been praising God for his almighty power and love. How can that not remind us that he is both able and willing to give us the good things we need if we ask him? The intercessions make sure that we take time to pray for all of the things Christians ought to pray for.

There is a difference in character between the intercessions of Morning Prayer and those of the evening. In the morning, the intercessions are more concerned with consecrating our day to God. They focus on asking for the grace and virtues we will need to live our day well. We ask God to keep us from sin, fill us with love for our neighbor, direct all our actions, and help us to bear wrongs patiently. In the evening, the intercessions make us look beyond our own needs. At Vespers, we pray for a wide array of people and situations: the pope, bishops and priests, religious, married couples, political leaders, farmers, the poor, the sick, those who mourn, widows and orphans, sinners, non-Christians, the imprisoned, the unemployed, an end to war, and last of all, every single day we pray for the dead.

It's an extensive list. I know a woman who says the evening intercessions are her favorite part of the Liturgy of the Hours because they give her the chance to pray for all the things we really *ought* to pray for but seldom do on our own, preoccupied as we are with our more immediate and personal needs. This is so true. And the good news is, the General Instruction gives us the option of adding our personal petitions, as well. It is appropriate to add these near the end, just prior to the final petition for the dead at the very end of the evening intercessions.

There are different methods of praying the petitions, depending on whether you are praying alone, with other people, or with a group that is led by a priest, deacon, or religious. Your breviary gives you the "material" you need for all methods, without explaining when to use what. This often leads to all options being used at once! According to the General Instruction, a leader may read both parts of the intercession, and the community respond with the unvarying refrain, which is similar to the "Lord, hear our prayer" that we use at Mass. Alternatively, the leader says the first half of the intercession, and the rest of the group prays the second half as their response, in which case no one uses the unvarying refrain. Here are examples of the two options:[11]

Option A

Priest or leader:

We give you thanks, Father, for the glories of creation,

—and for the even greater mystery of our redemption.

People:

Lord, hear our prayer.

Option B

Priest, leader, or group 1:

We give you thanks, Father, for the glories of creation,

Group 2:

—and for the even greater mystery of our redemption.[12]

What often happens in groups that aren't familiar with the General Instruction is that those who say the second half of the petition then respond to their own response with *Lord, hear our prayer.* It feels awkward, but they plow ahead, wanting to do what the breviary seems to be telling them to do. Hopefully, future editions of the breviary will make these options a bit clearer.

Praying individually? You may pray the intercessions any way you like. My own preference is Option B: to read the entire petition, then move on to the next one without the response. Sometimes my husband and I pray Lauds while in the car on the way to morning Mass. In this case, my husband will answer with the non-varying response after I read each petition.

Our Father

The Our Father has a place of honor at the end of the Intercessions. Therefore, the General Instructions note that the Lord's Prayer is solemnly recited by the Church three times a day: Morning Prayer, Evening Prayer, and the Mass of the day. If a priest is present, he may preface the Our Father with a short invitation similar to the one used at Mass. The Our Father should be said by everyone in its entirety, not split into parts as we do during the rosary.

Concluding Prayer

A concluding prayer "wraps up" each liturgical hour. These prayers will vary from the ordinary psalter prayers on feast days, Sundays throughout the year, and every day during the holy seasons. This concluding prayer is identical to the Collect (opening prayer) at the day's Mass for the Office of Readings during ordinary time and for Morning Prayer and Evening Prayer during the holy seasons and on feast days. This correspondence was especially noted when the new missal translations came out in 2011. A query was made: May we use the new translation of the collects when we conclude the Liturgy of the Hours? The United States bishops replied in the affirmative. This means those who care to do it should keep some kind of missal or daily Mass guide at hand until such a time when a new edition of the breviary is available. Alternatively, several of the online breviaries now include both the new and the old translations of the concluding prayer. The new translation of these prayers will appear in future editions of the breviary.

Closing Verse

Every liturgical hour has a short concluding verse. Like the opening verse (God, come to my assistance), it is said while making the Sign of the Cross. With the daytime Hours and the Office of Readings, this closing verse is optional when praying alone.

The closing verse brings the liturgical Hour to a fitting conclusion. It's a final petition for what matters most of all: God's protection in this life and salvation in the next. We've spent the few minutes that constitute a liturgical Hour fulfilling our highest purpose: to recognize and adore our Creator. We end this time by humbly asking for the gifts he most longs to give us.

Good to Know—With a Priest or With a Mass

If you are praying the Liturgy of the Hours with a group and a priest or deacon is leading, you will notice a few differences. It is his role to begin the introductory verse, to introduce the intercessions, to introduce the Our Father with words similar to those used at Mass, and to end with a final priestly blessing instead of the simple conclusion that is used in the absence of clergy.

There is also an authorized method to combine a liturgical Hour—generally Morning Prayer—with the celebration of Mass. Briefly, the psalmody is said at the beginning of Mass (replacing the penitential rite); the reading of Morning Prayer is omitted in favor of the readings of the day's Mass, and the intercessions of either Morning Prayer or the Mass of the day are used. The Mass proceeds as usual from that point, and Morning Prayer is picked up again after Communion, when the Canticle of Zechariah is said, and then the Mass proceeds to its conclusion. There are slight variations to this program when Daytime Prayer or Evening Prayer is combined with Mass at these later times of day.

You are more likely to experience the combination of Mass with a liturgical Hour when you visit a monastery or seminary, but occasionally this is done in parishes, as well.

CHAPTER SIX

Hour by Hour

You have seen in chapter four that each of the liturgical hours follows the same basic framework, whether it's the psalmody, readings, responsories, or prayers. Some are longer, some shorter. Morning and Evening Prayer have a few extra elements. The Office of Readings has two readings instead of one—and long ones at that. But beyond these variations, each of the Hours has a specific character or "personality." Each Hour has traits that make it appropriate to pray at the particular time of day that gives it its name. And each Hour has a specific application to the life of the Church and to your spiritual life.

Let's look at the hours in their "order of appearance" through the day, from morning to night.

Awaking the Dawn—Morning Prayer

Morning Prayer is one of the two principal Hours of the day on which the day's liturgy—and our own day—should hang. Hence, the Church's reference to Morning and Evening Prayer as the "hinges" of the liturgical day. That makes sense on the natural level. Our day's activity begins in the morning, and winds down in the evening. It is fitting to sanctify this beginning and ending of our daily work with liturgical prayer.

Although the entire Liturgy of the Hours is about offering to God a sacrifice of praise, no other Hour seems more praise-oriented than

Morning Prayer. It's Latin name—*Lauds*—means just that: praises. And this makes sense, because to the mind of the Church, every morning recalls the most amazing and glorious thing that ever happened: the resurrection of Jesus. We are often told that every Sunday is a "little Easter." In the Liturgy of the Hours, nearly every morning of the year, for a few minutes at least, is a little Easter. The idea of every morning commemorating the resurrection goes back to the earliest centuries.

The only appropriate way to recall Christ's passing from death to life is with the most joyful expressions of praise and thanks we can muster. We find it natural to associate the rising sun with the rising Son. Most of the psalms that refer to the dawn and the rising sun will be found in Morning Prayer. The Gospel canticle of Zechariah is perfect for the morning, speaking as it does of "the dawn from on high, that shines on those who dwell in darkness and the shadow of death." Psalm 19, the first half of which we pray on Monday of Week II, invites us first, in its literal meaning, to praise God for the beauty of the skies, and second, in its ancient Christian interpretation, to see the risen Christ in the sun that "comes forth like a bridegroom coming from his tent, rejoices like a champion to run his course."

Furthermore, we have something else for which to praise God: the new day he has given us. Many of the psalms used in Morning Prayer recall the dawn of creation. On Sunday mornings, in particular, the psalms and the canticles catalog the beauty and wonders of all the God has made. Morning Prayer reminds us to acknowledge, first thing each day, the two greatest gifts God has given us: creation and redemption, life and eternal life. In the end, nothing else really matters. Yes, life can be a vale of tears. Our sufferings great and small can wear us down. But each new day offers light for the body and the soul as we recall the fundamental reasons for the hope that is in us.

Midday Rest—Terce, Sext, and None

When is a liturgical hour *not* a liturgical hour?

When it's *three* liturgical hours. In other words, when it's Daytime Prayer. Since the revision of the liturgy by the Second Vatican Council, the expectation of the Church is that parish clergy, members of active religious orders, and laity who pray the Office will usually only have time for one of the three Daytime Hours (Mid-morning, Midday, Mid-afternoon). Hence, in church documents and in breviaries, one sees references to "Daytime Prayer" or "the Middle Hour." All three hours continue to exist in the liturgy, and all three remain in daily use for those whose religious vocation includes commitment to the complete Liturgy of the Hours. The rest of us are encouraged to use all three when the occasion permits: on retreats, for example, or on solemnities.

These three "little" Hours are named from their traditional time of day, which numbers the Hours using the biblical methods, where sunrise or 6 AM is considered the first hour of the day. So *Terce*, or third hour, is 9 AM; *Sext*, sixth hour, is noon; and *None*, ninth hour, is 3 PM. Perhaps the most delightful feature of these three Hours is that their prayers often recall specific events that took place, according to the Bible, at precisely those hours. So *Terce* often recalls that the Holy Spirit descended on the apostles in mid-morning: Remember the protest of Peter that they could not be drunk as it was "only the third hour of the day" (Acts 2:15)? *Sext*, or Midday Prayer, might recall Jesus's condemnation by Pilate (see John 19:14), his crucifixion (see Matthew 27:45), or Peter's vision in Acts 1:4. *None* or Mid-afternoon Prayer refers at times to the death of Jesus (see Mark 15:34), the appearance of the angel to Cornelius (see Acts 10:3), and the daily Jewish hour of Afternoon Prayer that the apostles observed in Jerusalem (see Acts 3:1). These reminders prompt mini-meditations on the events of salvation history.

At other times, the prayers of daytime recall not sacred events, but rather the purpose of the Middle Hour—and our own story in the life of the Church. For Daytime Prayer is above all meant to be a break from our daily work. It's an opportunity to stop our busyness, and—at least mentally—get away from the many things, great and small, important and petty, that demand our time and energy. This momentary pause for prayer is meant to give us the strength to then get back to work and complete our tasks faithfully, for his glory:

> God of mercy, this midday moment of rest is your welcome gift. Bless the work we have begun, make good its defects and let us finish it in a way that pleases you (Midday, Wednesday, Week II).

> Lord, help us to follow the example of your Son's patience and endurance. May we face all life's difficulties with confidence and faith (Mid-afternoon, Thursday, Week II).

The above quotes are from concluding prayers to the Daytime Hour. The special character of Daytime Prayer is also evident in the choice of the psalms. I could almost say the choice of the *psalm*, singular. Because for about twenty-two out of the twenty-eight days of the Daytime psalter, the psalmody consists partly or completely of sections of Psalm 119, which is the longest psalm in the Bible. It is divided into twenty two sections, each beginning with a letter of the Hebrew alphabet. It's theme: God's law and our response to it. Psalm 119 marvels that God has given us clear instructions for knowing right from wrong; it grieves that not everyone follows this life-giving path—and that sometimes these nonbelievers resent those who do follow it, making life rough for them. The psalmist begs God for increased discernment in order to understand the law more completely. In the midst of suffering, he finds consolation in the fact that God's law is a constant in his life.

Why is this lengthy eulogy of God's law so appropriate to this break in our workday? Think about it.

One thing we need in order to accomplish our daily work honorably is knowledge and application of God's law. From not cheating your employer with extended coffee breaks or stealing office supplies, to avoiding gossip, to willingly getting up from a comfortable chair *yet again* to attend to the needs of your child, our daily work is all about "doing the right thing." God's law, whether it's the Ten Commandments, the natural law he has written in our hearts, or the precepts of the Church, is precisely the magnetic pole towards which we must orient ourselves. These daily chunks of Psalm 119 right smack in the middle of our workday are exactly the reminders that we need.

These days people like to say, "I'm spiritual but not religious." The implication is that "spiritual" (whatever that means) is good, but "religious" is bad. Religion, in this view, means keeping a bunch of rules and regulations that stifle our freedom if we observe them and pass judgment on us if we don't. Psalm 119 stomps on this *zeitgeist*, presenting a relationship with divine law that is not a burden, but more of a love affair:

> I rejoice in the way of your precepts,
> as though all riches were mine
>
> …
>
> My soul is consumed with longing at all times for your decrees.
>
> …
>
> I will run in the way of your commands;
> you open wide my heart.
>
> …

In your commands I have found my delight;
these have I loved.

Truly, we need Psalm 119 to remind us that the pursuit of goodness during the daily nine-to-five routine is a beautiful thing, not drudgery.

Complementary Psalms

Those who find the time to pray more than one Daytime Hour will use the regular psalter for the first Daytime Hour they pray, but for the others turn to the complementary psalms at the end of the four-week psalter. (These psalms are also used for all the hours of Daytime Prayer on feasts and solemnities.) The complementary psalms are taken from a group known as the "gradual" psalms, or psalms of ascent. This is because, according to tradition, faithful Jews would sing Psalms 120 thru 134 as they "gradually" approached Jerusalem on pilgrimage. St. Benedict placed these short psalms in the Daytime Hours, because their brevity made them easy to memorize. Thus monks at work in the fields did not have to hurry to the chapel when the daytime bells were rung. Instead, they could pray these psalms where they were from memory.

Lighting the Lamps—Evening Prayer

Vespers, or Evening Prayer, is the other principle liturgical Hour. We greeted the dawn with Lauds, now we mark the setting of the sun with Vespers. Evening Prayer can bring several ideas to mind. It can recall the daily burnt offering made at sunset in the temple of Jerusalem as we make our own sacrifice of praise. With Evening Prayer, we thank God for the successful completion of the day's work and lay our hopes and sorrows at the feet of the Almighty:

Let my prayer be accepted as incense before you,
the raising of my hands like an evening oblation. (Psalm 141:2,
Evening Prayer I of Sunday, Week I)

Another Evening Prayer theme is light overcoming darkness. Traditionally, lighting the evening lamps was part of the Evening Prayer rubrics. We thank God for the light that protects us from the dangers of physical darkness, but more especially for the light of faith and grace that protects us from the evil one:

The Lord is my light and my help;
whom shall I fear? (Psalm 27, Wednesday, Week I).

Your word is a lamp for my steps,
and a light for my path. (Psalm 119, Sunday, Week II)

Let us give thanks to the Father
for having made you worthy
to share the lot of the saints
in light.
He rescued us from the power of darkness. (Colossians 1:12–
13, Wednesday, Week II)

Good to Know—Out of the Darkness
The constant availability of electric light has caused us to lose our appreciation for the gift of light that dispels evening's darkness. We only recapture this sense several times a year, for example, at the blessing of the new fire at the Easter Vigil, or, more practically, when we finally locate candles and matches during an evening power outage. It wouldn't be a bad idea to begin Sunday Vespers

on dark evenings by lighting a candle in a dark or dimly lit room. If you have blessed candles from the feast of the Presentation, this would be a good use for them.

Just as Morning Prayer recalls the Resurrection, Evening Prayer also recalls the death of Christ on the evening of Good Friday. However, the tone of the prayer is not to mourn, but to acclaim his victory on the cross. The canticles of Evening Prayer are all from the New Testament. These canticles are magnificent poetry, glorifying Christ for his salvific death, and also anticipating his final coming at the end of time:

We praise you, the Lord God Almighty,
who is and who was.
You have assumed your great power,
you have begun to reign (Revelation11:17, Thursday, Week II).

...obediently accepting even death,
death on a cross!
Because of this,
God highly exalted him
and bestowed on him the name
above every other name (Philippians 2:8–9, Sunday, Week III).

Worthy are you, O Lord,
to receive the scroll and break open its seals.
For you were slain;
with your blood you purchased for God
men of every race and tongue,

of every race and nation

…

Worthy is the Lamb that was slain

to receive power and riches,

wisdom and strength,

honor and glory and praise (Revelation 5:9, 12).

A Perfect End—Night Prayer

Compline means "completion." Night Prayer completes our day. It is bedtime prayer. Its psalms and canticles speak of confidence in God's love and protection for his sleeping children. The psalms and antiphons of Night Prayer are suitably brief for our tiredness. Night Prayer offers us comfort and reassurance:

I will lie down in peace and sleep comes at once,

for you alone, Lord, make me dwell in safety (Psalm.4, Saturday night).

Into your hands I commend my spirit (Psalm 31, responsory, every night).

Protect us, Lord, as we stay awake; watch over us as we sleep, that awake we may keep watch with Christ, and asleep, rest in his peace (antiphon for canticle of Simeon, every night).

Night holds no terror for me sleeping under God's wings (antiphon for Psalm 91, Sunday night). I will bless the Lord who gives me counsel, who even at night directs my heart (Psalm 16, Thursday night).

The readings of Night Prayer are brief, pithy, and memorable statements. Sunday night: Love God with all your heart and soul.

Monday night: God has planned that we achieve salvation through Jesus. Tuesday night: Be alert. Resist Satan. Wednesday night: Don't let the sun set on your anger.

We should pray Night Prayer with more than literal sleep in mind. We also pray it in anticipation of the final sleep of death—and receiving God's loving reassurance about that, as well. Indeed, the psalms of Tuesday and Friday's Night Prayer are of a more sorrowful type, meant to put us in mind of Gethsemane and give voice to our own sorrows or those of others. But that refrain of ultimate trust and abandonment to Mercy: "Into your hands" ties the whole day together into a package that we can give to him and forget about. Christ is with us. Always. Tomorrow is another day.

And if that's not enough to make us feel relaxed and safe, we finish Night Prayer with a Marian antiphon, calling on the Mother of God to tuck us into bed.

Wisdom of the Word and of the Saints—Office of Readings

For monks, the Office of Readings is for late night or extremely early morning. For the rest of us, it's whenever we want to do it. So it does not sanctify any one specific time of day. The character of this Office differs strongly from that of the others.

The name says it all. In the other liturgical Hours, psalmody takes the center stage. It's all about the "sacrifice of praise" that we offer, with Christ, to the Father. Not so in the Office of Readings. Yes, the psalms are there as usual, but one gets the feeling that in this case, they are there to prepare us for the main event, which is the readings. We come to this Office not so much to praise as to learn. We come seeking wisdom both from God's Word and from our elder brothers and sisters, the fathers, doctors, and saints of the Church.

We know it's important to read the Bible—on a daily basis if possible. We know that there's so much to learn from the great saints and Christian teachers of the past. But most of us also know from hard experience that plans to read through the entire Bible starting with Genesis rarely make it anywhere close to Revelation. Neither do many of us ever get around to a serious study of the fathers of the Church.

But here, in the office of readings, the Church gives us manageable daily portions of both Scripture and saints, arranged according the feasts and seasons of the liturgical year. The first reading usually follows one book of the Bible for several days or weeks at a time. Advent gives us a sizable portion of Isaiah; Lent takes us through most of Exodus, and Eastertide takes us on a tour of the book of Revelation.

Occasionally, the second reading is a direct commentary on the first. Other times, the second reading comments more generally on a theme related to the liturgical season. During Ordinary Time, it might be a commentary on the Gospel, the psalms, or just about any aspect of Christian faith. The list of authors of these readings is a veritable Christian hall of fame: Athanasius, Augustine, Chrysostom, Eusebius, Polycarp, and Leo the Great are just a few of the fathers represented. Although heavily weighted towards these most ancient teachers, the Office of Readings also introduces us to more recent ones, whom the Church has named as its "doctors." This list begins in the Middle Ages and proceeds through the centuries: Bernard, Thomas Aquinas, Catherine of Siena, Francis de Sales, Anthony of Padua, Teresa.

On saints' feast days, the second reading usually sets aside the mighty fathers and doctors. Instead, the saint of the day often speaks to us. These are among the most fascinating readings because they are often highly personal glimpses into the souls of the saints. We read excerpts from the prison diary kept by St. Perpetua as she approached the day of her martyrdom. St. Gregory the Great talks about how difficult he finds it to live a holy life amidst all the administrative and social duties he has as Pope. St. Louis X, King of France, gives advice to the son who will reign after him.

Using the Office of Readings used to require the purchase of the four-volume breviary. Given the $100-plus price tag, this was a barrier for many. Nowadays, adding this hour is a simple matter for anyone with a computer—and even more convenient for those with a tablet or smart phone.

Of course, there is always the difficulty of fitting the Office of Readings into your schedule, especially if you are already just barely squeezing in Morning and Evening Prayer. Again, start small: Maybe consider doing the Office of Readings as your extra spiritual practice just for Lent. And ask God to help you find the time.

Perhaps we should stop seeing the Office of Readings as "that really *long* liturgical Hour with those two *long* readings," and instead start thinking of it as "that really compact, efficient daily prayer that makes it possible for me to pray, read Scripture, and read the best of the writings of the saints, all in less than a half hour."

Good to Know—Ordinary Catholics Rave About the Office of Readings

Nearly everyone has had the experience of reading the Scriptures and coming across a verse that "had their name on it"—a verse you needed to see that day that spoke to your heart. It's something like that with the second reading in the Office of Readings. An idea gets articulated exactly as you need it to be. A metaphor clarifies

an entire murky problem. A saint leaves you dazed with the beauty of holiness.
—*Harold*

I wouldn't know where to start reading the Fathers of the Church [on my own], and this way I have a place to jump in.
—*Naomi*

The Scriptures chosen [for the Office of Readings] seem to be the best of the Bible—books we should be familiar with…. The readings from the Fathers are not only complementary to the Bible readings, but they offer a continuous education in our faith. To see that the faith has been taught so consistently for centuries just boggles the mind. Reading and reflecting on them is not only a spiritual exercise but a great learning tool.
—*Lenny*

CHAPTER SEVEN

Praying the Calendar: Seasons and Feasts

You are reading this book because you are interested in the Liturgy of the Hours. That probably means you are fairly devout, committed, and well-informed about the Faith. So you are most likely familiar with the concept of the liturgical year and the calendar of saints. You've noticed that the Mass focuses on very specific Gospel events during Advent, Christmas, Lent, and Easter. You've observed the changing colors of the priest's vestments at those times. You know that there are holy days scattered throughout the year and that each saint has a feast day. Let's look at how this cycle—and gift—of the liturgical year dovetails with the Liturgy of the Hours.

The Year of Grace

The yearly liturgical cycle, like the changing seasons in nature, is a gift from God designed to fit with the needs of human nature. On the one hand, we like a measure of variety in our lives. We delight in seeing the first robin and crocus as spring begins. We can't wait for the warmth of summer and its promise of lazy days in the sun, while steaks sizzle on the grill. We are glad when the evenings grow cool and visions of colorful foliage thrill us on the morning commute. Even people who hate the cold of winter and fear icy roads will still grudgingly admit that the first snowfall is a thing of beauty.

At the same time, we also crave familiarity and continuity. We welcome back the spring, summer, and fall not only because they are different, but because they are also old friends. Much as we might want a long winter to end, we'd be alarmed if it gave way to a new, unknown season, where the sky turned bright green, periodic showers of pebbles fell to earth, and tiny geysers popped out on our lawns. No, we love seasonal change because, in ways, it *doesn't* change. It gives us recurring, familiar variety.

The liturgical year gives a similar framework and focus to our worship and prayer. Seasons of penance and preparation (Advent, Lent) give way to seasons of feast and rejoicing (Christmas, Easter), as we mark the events of salvation history. Next comes the long vacation of Ordinary Time, and then it all begins again. Sprinkled throughout the year are feasts and memorials to honor our heroes, the saints. What the seasons in nature do for us psychologically, the liturgical year does for our spiritual lives.

For Catholics whose liturgical experience is limited to Sunday Mass, the strength of this effect will depend on how well they reflect on that Mass for the next six days. Those who are able to attend one or more daily Masses will find themselves more thoroughly connected to the liturgical year. Alternatively, the daily use of the Liturgy of the Hours can immerse us in the holy seasons and feasts on a daily, even hourly, basis.

Good to Know—There's Nothing Ordinary About Ordinary Time

The liturgical year has two stretches of "ordinary time," comprising a total of thirty-four weeks. Six to eight of these weeks occur as a break between the end of Christmastide and the start of Lent. The rest come in a long stretch between Pentecost and the first Sunday of Advent. People often think that these Sundays and weekdays are termed "ordinary" in contrast to the pageantry of the holy seasons. It's an easy mistake to make, since we certainly feel a sense of returning to "ordinary life" for example, after the Christmas season has come to an end. In fact, however, the term *ordinary* in the liturgical year is not meant to imply *routine, normal,* or *uneventful.* It mainly refers to the Sundays being numbered, in *order.* While the focus of the holy seasons (Advent through Pentecost) is Christ saving us, ordinary time celebrates Christ leading us to all truth.

Parts of the Breviary for the Liturgical Seasons

When a newcomer looks at the table of contents of a breviary, he is typically floored by all the headings and doesn't know where to begin. The tutorial resources listed in chapter three will make everything more clear, but for now, here's a quick guide to the parts of the breviary that you will need most often.

• **The Four-Week Psalter**—You will use the psalter nearly every day of the year. Although it's in the middle third of your breviary (around page 700 in the one-volume edition), you will usually begin each liturgical Hour in this section. On weekdays in ordinary time, you won't use anything else but the psalter for morning, evening, and daytime prayer. It is the foundation of the Liturgy of the Hours.

• **Proper of Seasons**—If it's Advent, Christmastide, Lent, or the Easter season, you use the psalter only as far as the end of the psalmody. Then you'll turn to the front third of your breviary, the Proper of Seasons, and turn to whatever season, week, and day it is. The rest of the Hour, from reading to concluding prayer, is there. For Christmas Day and the Easter Triduum, the Proper of Seasons contains the entire Office. You will also make use of the Proper of Seasons on every Sunday of the year. Even in Ordinary Time, Sundays have special Gospel canticle antiphons and concluding prayers in this section. The Proper of Seasons also contains the full Offices for the solemnities that occur during Ordinary Time: Trinity Sunday, Corpus Christi, Christ the King, and also the Friday Solemnity of the Sacred Heart.

• **Proper of Saints**—Found in the last third of your breviary, the Proper of Saints lists all solemnities, feasts, and memorials of Mary and the saints, plus a couple of feasts of Our Lord that do not fall on Sundays. These are all listed in calendar order. The Proper includes a short explanation of the feast or the saint. It gives you any antiphons, readings, or prayers that are unique to the day, and it directs you to the Common that may be needed.

• **Commons**—Think of these as generic offices for different types of saint's days: holy women, holy men, martyrs, apostles, doctors of the church, religious, etc. There is also an Office for the dedication of a church, a common of the Blessed Virgin Mary, and the Office of the Dead.

Good to Know—Which Week in the Psalter Am I on?

How does a beginner figure out which week of the psalter is currently in use? Lacking the printed yearly guide or Internet access, you can figure this out yourself with your parish calendar. All you need to know is your four times multiplication table. Look at the most recent Sunday on your calendar. It will say what Sunday in Ordinary Time it is. If by chance it's a multiple of four (4, 8, 12, 16...) then you should use Week IV of the Psalter. If it's a multiple of four minus one, (3, 7, 11, 15…) then you want Week III of the psalter. If it's a multiple of four minus two, use Week II. Four minus three? Week I.

The four weeks of Advent correspond with Weeks I thru IV of the psalter. The six weeks of Lent correspond to Weeks I thru IV, then I and II again. The same situation applies to the weeks of the Easter season.

Sorting Through Solemnities, Feasts, and Memorials

Catholics casually refer to everything from All Saints' Day to the name-day of their patron saint as "feast days." We also use the term "holy day" to refer to days besides Sunday when we are obligated to attend Mass. Technically, there are several different categories of special days on the liturgical calendar. These names designate the level of importance of each day, and indicate which prayers we must (or may) use in either the Mass or in the Liturgy of the Hours. Here are some explanations for these terms.

Solemnities

These are the holiest days in honor of Jesus, Mary, and some of the greatest saints. Some of these are the familiar holy days of obligation, although this designation is made by individual bishops' conferences or by dioceses, and they vary greatly from one country to another. Other solemnities occur on Sundays after Pentecost (Most Holy Trinity, Corpus Christi). There are several solemnities on which we are not obliged to attend Mass, for example, the feast of St. Joseph (March 19), the Annunciation (March 25), and the Birth of St. John the Baptist (June 24). If you do attend Mass on these days, you will notice that the Mass is said like a Sunday Mass, including the Gloria, the Creed, and three readings.

In the Liturgy of the Hours, solemnities are celebrated similarly to Sundays. There is an Evening Prayer I on the evening before Sunday, and the Office of Vigils may be said. The *Te Deum* is also added to the Office of Readings. Morning Prayer generally uses Sunday of Week I for the psalmody. For everything else the solemnity has its own office in either the Proper of Seasons or the Proper of Saints.

If a solemnity occurs on a Sunday in Ordinary Time, its Mass and Office take precedence over that of the Sunday. If a solemnity occurs on a Sunday during Advent or Lent, it does not take precedence, but instead is celebrated on the following Monday.

Feasts

Feasts are of lesser prominence than solemnities. If a feast occurs on a Sunday (unless it is a feast of Our Lord), the regular Sunday Office takes precedence. Likewise, a feast is not celebrated if it falls on Ash Wednesday, on a solemnity, during holy week, or during the octave of Easter. Feasts still honor important saints and events in the lives of Jesus and Mary. Some examples are the Conversion of St. Paul (January 25), the Chair of St. Peter (February 22), the feasts of each of the other apostles, the Holy Archangels (September 29), the Presentation of Our Lord (February 2), the Transfiguration (August 6), and the Birth of Mary (September 8).

Feasts are celebrated in the Liturgy of the Hours in the same way as solemnities, using whatever is provided in the Proper of Saints and/or the Commons. (You will not use the current weekday in the psalter.) Unlike solemnities, feasts do not have an Evening Prayer I, the one exception being when a feast of Our Lord falls on a Sunday.

Memorials

Memorials are the next category of importance for liturgical celebrations. There are two subcategories of memorials: obligatory and optional. In American breviaries, the word *memorial* appears beneath the saint's name in the Proper when there is an obligatory memorial. If no designation appears beneath the saint's name, it signifies that the memorial is optional.

There is no difference in how either of these two subcategories of memorials are celebrated, except that the optional memorials/commemorations are, well, optional. You may skip them altogether if you prefer to just use the current weekday in the psalter.

To celebrate a memorial, use the current weekday in the psalter for the psalms and antiphons. After that, continue either with the weekday in the psalter *or* use one of the Commons, substituting any elements that appear in the Proper of Saints for that day. Often, these saint-specific elements in the Proper may be no more than the concluding prayer, but sometimes they may include antiphons, readings, and responsories. It seems that the saints most likely to have a more personalized Proper are the ones who have been revered from ancient times, such as Saints Anne and Joachim, St. Agnes, St. Mary Magdalene, and St. Lawrence. The majority of memorials only give a concluding prayer for the saint in the Proper.

Memorials, whether optional or obligatory, are not celebrated when they fall on the same days of precedence listed above for feasts. In addition, you do not celebrate memorials during Advent weekdays from December 17 onwards, during the octave of Christmas, or on weekdays during Lent.

There is a handy chart on page 37 of the *Christian Prayer* breviary, titled "Format of the Offices." It offers, in outline style, a summary of much of the information discussed above about saints' days.

When Is a Memorial Not a Memorial?

The listings in the Proper of Saints in your breviary are those of the universal Roman calendar. But every national bishops' conference, diocese, and religious order has its own liturgical calendar, or *ordo*, which will contain variations from the universal calendar. There will be saints and feasts that are of greater interest to these specific populations. For example, the feast of Our Lady, Mother of Africa, is celebrated on April 30 on that continent. St. Bernadette is a memorial in France that is not celebrated in the United States. Our Lady of Guadalupe (December 12), a mere optional memorial in Europe and Africa, has the status of a feast in North and South America. It should be no surprise that the feast day of St. Francis is a solemnity rather than a memorial for Franciscans, and that of Ignatius Loyola is a solemnity for the Jesuits.

What significance does this have for the ordinary lay person who prays the Liturgy of the Hours? First, if ever you join in liturgical prayer at a monastery, you may experience times when your own breviary doesn't "work" since the monks or nuns are using completely different prayers. What appears to be a weekday of Ordinary Time in your breviary is actually the memorial of Blessed Unknown So and So among your monastic friends. Now you will know why.

In addition, since the General Instruction encourages laity to adapt the Liturgy of the Hours to our own needs, it seems that we, too, could occasionally celebrate the days of favorite saints with greater solemnity than the universal calendar gives them. If you have great devotion to St. Anthony or St. Therese and wish to celebrate their memorials as feasts, using the entire Common rather than the current weekday in the psalter, then go ahead.

Good to Know—Uncommon Commons

The Common of the Blessed Virgin Mary is used in whole or in part for various solemnities, feasts, and memorials of Our Lady. It also may be used as a Votive (alternate) Office on any Saturday in Ordinary Time, assuming no obligatory memorial, feast, or solemnity occurs on that day. This is because, in the Church's tradition, Saturday has always been considered a day to honor the Blessed Virgin.

The Office for the Dead, found at the end of the "commons" section in your breviary, is used in its entirety on All Soul's Day. You may also pray it on the day you attend someone's funeral, when you learn of someone's death, or on the anniversary of a loved one's death. The Office for the Dead may also be used occasionally as a Votive Office on weekdays, subject to the same conditions listed above for the common of the Blessed Virgin Mary. It is a good way to carry out our duty of praying for all the souls of the faithful departed.

PART THREE

It's one thing to know how to find your place in book—or know about repeating the antiphon after the Glory Be. Or even to know how to juggle common and psalter on a feast day.

It's something else entirely to enter into the *spirit* of the psalter. Some people grasp it intuitively from their very first experience of Morning, Evening, or Night Prayer. Others have some difficulty appreciating many of the psalms. Sometimes the mood or imagery of any given psalm can seem at best irrelevant—or at worst downright jarring—to one's ideas of what prayer ought to be. If that is how you have felt, please don't be discouraged. The Psalms as prayer can be an acquired taste. But the acquisition is well worth the effort.

In this final section, we'll view several beautiful aspects of the Liturgy of the Hours through the lens of some common complaints and highlight some strategies for making your journey of praying the Hours a personal and rewarding one. For a more thorough and more eloquent teaching on this topic, I urge everyone to read—a little bit at a time—the General Instruction on the Liturgy of the Hours. This appears in its entirety in Volume I of the four-volume breviary and in selections in the one-volume breviary. It can also be found online.

CHAPTER EIGHT

Common Quibbles With the Psalms

Why Does God Need So Much Praise?

This book has spoken of the Liturgy of the Hours as a sacrifice of praise. The assumption is that everyone already understands that praising God is the highest form of prayer—indeed, among the greatest of human actions. But given our earthly experience of praise, we might find ourselves hesitating on this point.

There was certainly a time when I wondered why we were supposed to praise God so much. Was the Lord eternally fishing for compliments, like a once-beautiful woman now past her prime? So egotistical that he needed us telling him how wonderful he was every single day? Would he be offended if we didn't remember to commend him for his goodness on a regular basis? I knew that God couldn't really be like that, but figured this was one of those mysteries, like the Trinity, that we would only understand completely in heaven.

Fortunately, it's not so great a mystery that we can't understand it pretty well right now. Simply put, God does not demand our praise because *he* needs it, but because *we* need it. It is for *our* benefit, not *his*. If the whole world neglected to ever utter a single word of praise to God, he would not be hurt or diminished in any way. But we, the non-praisers, would be sadly crippled.

Praise—call it admiration or appreciation—is the most natural response in the world to beauty, truth, and goodness. You are not in the least worried about offending a beautiful sunset by not praising it. On the contrary, you just can't help it. Your heart leaps, and words such as, "Wow! That's incredible!" come to your lips. And then—this is important—you aren't satisfied with having praised the sunset by yourself. You open the door to the house and call to your spouse and children, "Quick! Come see the sunset before it's gone! Isn't that amazing! Look at that red streak over there. The golden border on top of the purple. Get the camera!" Indeed, if the kids only grunted, shrugged their shoulders, and turned back to their video games, you would probably be upset with them. You would worry—if this kind of response was habitual—that their sense of beauty was seriously impaired. You might take steps to correct it, perhaps cutting down on gaming time, initiating regular family nature hikes, or having them checked for color-blindness.

There are many things that we—according to our interests and tastes—find praiseworthy. Every club or magazine or website devoted to a sport, breed of dog, hobby, artist, author, or actor is largely a vehicle for fans to say to one another, "Isn't this fantastic! Look at this or that new angle I've noticed! I can't wait until the next new amazing thing related to our favorite subject happens! Don't you agree that this is important, worthwhile, exciting?"

God, our Creator and Redeemer, the answer to the heart's deepest longings, is obviously the most worthy object of our praise. When we recognize our place in the universe—as mere creatures, and fallen ones at that, who have been miraculously elevated to the status of sons and daughters—praise of God is the only fitting response. (And that praise, just as with the sunset, is largely composed of inviting others to praise him, as well.) To not recognize this is to be spiritually disabled. And disabled we are, even to the last day of our lives on earth. Being fallen, it is often much easier to say, "Wow! Fantastic!" about the football play we can see than about the God we cannot see.

Yet by continually praising God with the words of the Psalms, we are training ourselves for the time when praise will be pure delight as we see him face-to-face. In his book *Reflections on the Psalms*, C.S. Lewis says that, "In commanding us to glorify him, God is inviting us to enjoy him." He describes our efforts at praise while on earth in this way:

> When we carry out our "religious duties" we are like people digging channels in a waterless land, in order that when at last the water comes it may find them ready.... There are happy moments, even now, when a trickle creeps along the dry beds; and happy souls to whom this happens often.[13]

The Psalter Is So Jewish!

No, this is not the complaint of an anti-Semite. It's the statement of a normal person who doesn't see the point in praying so often about the temple, burnt offerings, or the Mosaic law. After all, we are people of the new covenant. Why dwell so much on the old? Take this example, not of a psalm, but from a canticle we use every fourth Tuesday morning. Here, Azariah, a devout Jew living in exile in Babylon, is mourning the loss of all the pillars of his religion:

> We have in our day no prince, prophet, or leader,
> no holocaust, sacrifice, oblation, or incense,
> no place to offer first fruits, to find favor with you.
> (Daniel 3:38)

Why does the Church want us to pray these lines? After all, the one perfect holocaust, sacrifice, and oblation has been made. We can tap into it every day of the week at the nearest Catholic church. What does Azariah's complaint have to do with us? Plenty, actually.

The people of Israel are our elder brothers in the Faith. The phrase "God's people" means both us and them. So this is *our* history. Knowing that we now have the one sacrifice for all should make us appreciate even more what Azariah was mourning about. It should make us all the more glad that the terrible lack he spoke of has since been supplied in abundance and all the more hopeful that all our Jewish siblings will one day recognize their Savior.

Beyond that, we can always profit from praying with the vocabulary of the Old Testament by meditating on Jesus as he read and prayed these passages. What might he have been thinking as he recited these lines about no holocaust or place to offer it? Perhaps he reflected that he would be the holocaust and Calvary would be the place of offering. Listening to Jesus as he prays the Scriptures of his people helps us see the significance of that which has passed away and that which has been fulfilled.

Begin to recognize our connection to the people of Israel. Remember that Jesus is the Son of David and the psalms were his prayer. Then, all the Jewish details in the psalter will enhance your prayer rather than distract you from it.

But My Soul Isn't Filled With Evils!

It's a bright sunny morning. Your wonderful husband and your adorable, healthy children have just left for work and school. Your exercise and diet program is going well. Life is good. You sit down with your coffee and crack open the breviary. It's Tuesday of Week II in the psalter.

You read Psalm 43:

Defend me, O God, and plead my cause against a godless nation.

From deceitful and cunning men rescue me, O God.
Since you, O God are my stronghold, why have you rejected
me?
Why do I go mourning, oppressed by the foe?

"I don't feel like this!" you think to yourself. No one's oppressing me.
I'm not in mourning. I'm overwhelmed with God's blessings. This
psalm just doesn't work for me. Why should I pray it?"

A few months later, the opposite thing happens. It's a Sunday
morning, and the psalter is wild with joy, thanksgiving, and all-around
praise of God for all the wonderful things he'd done for his people. The
problem is that life for you at the moment is lousy. The twenty-four-
hour stomach bug is raging through your family, and you know that
you are next. The credit card bill is way too high. Your husband might
fall victim to the next round of layoffs. Life is not so good right now.

"I don't feel like this at all!" you think to yourself. "How can I rejoice
and praise God when things are so bad? What is the point of praying
these psalms? All they do is tempt me to resentment. Why should I
pray them?"

Yes, it might be easier to refer to one of those Bible Society bookmarks
that says, "When God seems far away, read Psalm X. When you are
worried, pray Psalm Y. To thank God for his blessings, see Psalm Z."
Just cherry-pick the book of Psalms according to your mood and your
need.

But instead, the Church gives us daily marching orders: "Here's how
the Body of Christ is praying today. Make this prayer your own." But
how do we manage that when the prayers are not in sync with our
feelings or situation in life?

One obvious answer is that there are probably just as many occasions
when the psalms of the day's prayer do, in fact, apply perfectly to your

situation. Times when a verse in a psalm, an antiphon, or a reading speaks to you as if God had arranged it to appear that day just for you. So let the Highly Relevant days cancel out the Highly Discordant days and just get on with it. To use a cliché, it's not about *you*.

Or maybe it *is* about you—insofar as you are a member of Christ's body on earth, the Catholic Church. We are supposed to be spiritually bonded to one another, with Christ as our head. If the day's prayers do not fit your emotional state, you can be sure they do fit that of many of your one billion brothers and sisters in Christ.

Reading a psalm of woe when you are cheerful? Pray it in union with the poor, the sick, and the unemployed. Pray it with the many Christians who face persecution, imprisonment, and martyrdom in nations oppressed by atheistic communism or radical Islam. Pray it for your sister's friend who is on pregnancy bed rest while having to manage several small children. Pray it for unborn children in danger of abortion and their conflicted mothers. Pray it for the co-worker whose wife just left him. It's very easy to find something to do with the psalms of sorrow, regardless of your own feelings.

Or take it to the next level. Apply a suffering psalm to the Church as a whole. The Bride of Christ is under attack in so many ways. From the outside, by hostile governments and social trends. From within, by unfaithful leaders and clergy. And from ourselves, whenever we undermine the Christian way of life by our own poor example.

And turn it all around on the days when psalms of triumph and thanksgiving don't mesh with your temporarily bleak mood. The Psalms give us reasons to rejoice—the beauty of the earth, the mercy of God—that are always there despite our present problems. God created us. He redeemed us. He promises eternal life. What else, in the end, really matters? These psalms remind us of hope amidst our tears.

The Psalms Can Be So Violent!

"I don't like those verses that talk about war and vengeance and asking God to squash one's enemies like bugs. I mean, some psalms, like Psalm 23, are really beautiful, but these other ones—they're kind of mean-spirited. Aren't we supposed to love our enemies, and be peaceful and forgiving?"

Indeed, there are few things more jarring to the Divine Office beginner than some of the hatred for enemies and the triumphant gloating of the victor than what we find in the psalms. King David doesn't just thank God for victory. He savors every detail of his enemies' despair and defeat. On Thursday, Week I, for example, the Office of readings gives us the last half of Psalm 18:

> I pursued and overtook my foes, never turning back til they were slain.
> I smote them so they could not rise; they fell beneath my feet.
>
> …
>
> They cried, but there was no one to save them;
> they cried to the Lord, but in vain.
> I crushed them fine as dust before the wind;
> trod them down like dirt in the streets…
>
> …
>
> Foreign nations came to me cringing.

Pretty harsh, isn't it?

Now let's take a look at that paragon of peace and goodness, Psalm 23. Every Christian loves this psalm for its imagery of pastures and still waters—and the comforting thought of God being with us even in the "valley of the shadow of death." But C.S. Lewis has pointed out that even this psalm contains a petty, vengeful little dig against enemies. Remember? "You prepare a table before me *in the sight of my foes.*" Apparently, God's gifts are all the sweeter when our deprived enemies have to watch us enjoy them. Not exactly a Christian attitude. So what do we do with violence, hatred, and revenge, large and small, in the psalms?

Here's what we *don't* have to do. We don't have to pretend that the psalmist was personally justified in his every attitude and action, just because he is a biblical hero. Indeed, it is instructive to see just how very imperfect the saints of the Old Testament could be. We don't have to be a combination of historian and moral theologian, determining which battles each psalm refers to and which of these were "just wars" and which ones were not.

What we have to do is figure out how to apply these warlike, violent, or vengeful verses to our prayer and that of the Church. Here are some ideas:

• Imagine you have just made some strides towards overcoming the worst of your faults. You know—the one you have to mention every single time you go to confession. The one that never seems to improve. Suddenly, through a combination of grace and grit, you have almost entirely overcome this thing. In fact, you are making strides in the opposing virtue. Wouldn't the victory boast of Psalm 18 express perfectly your feelings towards the evil inclinations you have crushed— and towards the evil spirits that have tempted you for years? Might you not happily imagine Satan's dismay at your victory?

• Imagine reading in the news of some impressive victory for the pro-life movement. Or some impressive statistics about the growth of the Church in, say, Africa. Again, these psalm verses might be just the thing to celebrate success against the forces of error and death, would they not?

• Imagine Our Lord praying this psalm and anticipating his own victory over sin and death. For the cross was the battlefield on which he triumphed and Satan the enemy whom he crushed.

In other words, to pray these violent psalms well, it helps to know your enemy. A little reflection will show that there are entities—evil spirits or just our own sinful inclinations—that we should be happy to crush, smite, and squash like bugs. We can pray these psalms with reference to these, both in our personal lives and that of the Church. We are also praying the prayer of Jesus in his fight to the death with Satan and his triumph over sin.

Good to Know—Toned-Down Psalter

Recognizing that the faithful might have a hard time with some of the most vengeful psalms, the Church removed three of them from the breviary in its Vatican II revision (look up Psalms 58, 83, and 109 in your Bible). In addition, a few verses from some of the other psalms have also been eliminated from the psalter because the Church deems them "somewhat harsh in tone." Before Vatican II, when the office was said in Latin, the graphic violence of these psalms was perhaps not so glaring. But imagine praying Psalm 58 in English: asking God to break the teeth of the wicked, to make them "dissolve into slime," and then declaring that good people will rejoice to see vengeance done. Or verse 9 of Psalm 137, where the Jews living in exile are called blessed if they can manage to kill a few Babylonian babies. This editing of the psalter for the breviary is considered controversial: Some argue that we can apply these passages to our struggle against evil, just as we do all the other violent passages. For instance, St. Augustine had no trouble "spiritualizing" that line about the Babylonian babies. He said we should think of this verse as an analogy for killing off our small faults before they grow into mortal sins. But whatever our personal opinions are about these edits to the psalter, we should accept the Church's decision.

CHAPTER NINE

More Help for Making the Liturgy of the Hours Your Own

How to Complain to God in Three Easy Steps

I used to think it was wrong to complain to the Lord. Perhaps I had overdosed on those stories of saints who are portrayed as positively craving new opportunities to suffer for the love of God, bursting into rhapsodies of delight at each new illness, inconvenience, and disappointment. So when the thought crossed my mind in times of trouble—"Lord, what on earth were you thinking to let this happen to me?"—I'd feel guilty afterward.

Yet, the psalmists complained plenty. They go on in great detail about how bad life is at the moment, and ask God why he hasn't fixed things yet. They tell God that they don't understand how he could work so many miracles in the past but rarely seems to do so anymore. They point out that nonbelievers are suggesting that maybe God is not so great if he allows such disasters to happen to his followers.

We can't dismiss this by saying, "That was the Old Testament. Christians have sanctifying grace, and now our suffering has redemptive value. Therefore we should accept it without complaint." Let's not forget that the Psalms were the prayers that Jesus prayed. As he was dying, he cried to his Father with the ultimate complaint from Psalm

22, "My God, my God, why have your forsaken me?" We can assume he was giving us an example to follow. And so is the Church in making the Psalms its official daily prayer.

What you will find in virtually all the psalms of sorrow and woe is a pattern of complaint-with-trust. A completely natural and honest outpouring of grievance is followed up by expressions of profound hope and confidence in God's will. Look in your Bible at Psalm 42, 43, or the one from which Jesus's cry of desolation came, Psalm 22. There you will find that primal cry in times of disaster: "Why, why, why are you allowing this to happen?" But then, after the storm of grief, a calm of not just resignation, but trust:

> Hope in God, I will praise him yet again,
> my saving presence and my God. (Psalm 42:12 and 43:5)

> And I will come to the altar of God,
> to God, my joy and gladness.
> To you will I give thanks on the harp,
> O God, my God. (43:4)

> And my soul shall live for him,
> my offspring serve him.
> They shall tell of the Lord to generations to come,
> declare his saving justice to peoples yet unborn:
> "These are the things the Lord has done." (22:31–32)

Now that Christ has defeated sin and death, our own sufferings, joined to his, do indeed have meaning. Any pain, from a stubbed toe to a cancer diagnosis, from a lost wedding ring to a lost job, can be offered to God in union with Christ's passion. And thus we are privileged, as members of his body, to save souls along with him. But that doesn't mean we can't cry out in our pain and bewilderment and desolation—that we can't beg God to take it away even as we offer it up.

The Psalms give us a foolproof formula for speaking to the Lord of our sorrows: Complain. Trust. Repeat.

Scriptural Exegesis for Beginners

The Liturgy of the Hours is overwhelmingly scriptural. Therefore, the more you know about how to understand Scripture, the more interesting and fruitful your prayer will be. There are four traditional ways, or senses, of understanding Sacred Scripture: the *literal* sense, the *allegorical* sense, the *moral* sense, and the *anagogical* sense. I'll briefly explain each of these with reference to Psalm 144, which appears in the psalter in Evening Prayer of Thursday, Week IV. Take a look at it in your Bible or breviary.

1. Literal Sense. This means reading Scripture as it was plainly intended by its human author. We can see that the psalmist, in this case King David, is praising God for giving him the strength to overcome his enemies in battle. He marvels that the mighty Lord of heaven cares about man at all. David asks the Lord to save him from foes who threaten to overwhelm him. He then asks that God bless his people with freedom and prosperity. We can admire David's humility and trust in God as we read the psalm literally.

2. Allegorical Sense. How does this psalm apply to Christ and the mystery of redemption—also known as the Christological sense? This book has already spoken frequently about this sense of interpreting the psalms because it is central to appreciating the Liturgy of the Hours. The caption above Psalm 144 in the breviary does the work for us: "Christ learned the art of warfare when he overcame the world, as he said: 'I have overcome the world'" (St. Hilary). We think of Jesus engaged in spiritual battle during the temptations in the desert, when casting out demons, and during his passion.

3. Moral Sense. How does this psalm apply to the Christian life—and to me in particular? Taking my cue from the allegorical meaning, I too can pray this psalm as a way of acknowledging my need for God's grace when engaged in spiritual warfare.

4. Anagogical Sense. How does the Scripture put us in mind of heaven as our final goal? Verses three and four of Psalm 144 remind us both of the briefness of life and God's care for us:

> Lord, what is man that you regard him,
>> the son of man that you keep him in mind,
> man who is merely a breath,
> whose days are like a passing shadow?

So here, we might reflect on the fact that our lives don't really end after the shadow of earthly life passes and rejoice that we are offered eternal life.

One caveat: Unless you have a literal, sixty-minute hour or more to spare for each liturgical Hour, don't try to find each of the four senses of scriptural meaning in every verse you read. Or even every psalm. This is the recipe for mental exhaustion. If you are a typical person with a job to get to, children to care for, a lawn to mow, a car to wash, and emails to answer, then you don't have the time to parse each psalm of each Hour in this way. My advice is to just keep the four senses of Scripture in the back of your mind without trying to use them all the time. The literal sense, of course, will come to you without effort if you read the psalm with attention; it's the plain sense of what you are reading. If you are moved to look beyond the literal, then ask yourself one of these questions: What is God telling me (moral sense)? What does this say about Christ or the Church (allegorical sense)? How does this help me think of my final purpose and end (anagogical sense)?

Remember that the subtitles, captions, and psalm prayers will help you with interpretation. As the months and years of faithfully praying the psalter roll by, you will find that your own ability to interpret the Psalms according to the four senses becomes, well, a sixth sense! On a good day, these layers of meaning will present themselves without too much effort on your part.

Good To Know—Finding the Minutes for the Hours

As ordinary Catholics, we don't have monastery bells reminding us to pray several times a day. And if we did, we'd often be unable to heed them, what with deadlines at work, crying children, home repairs, emergency grocery runs, and trips to kids' activities. Everything clamors for our attention more forcefully than that quiet little breviary. This is true of any kind of prayer—or for that matter, any new habit you want to establish, whether it's Bible reading, practicing the piano, menu planning, or working out. It takes motivation, creativity, and perseverance. The fact that you have read this far shows that you are motivated. Here are a few ideas that might help.

• **Start small.** Beginners who decide that nothing less than morning, daytime, evening, night prayer *and* Office of Readings will happen every day, starting tomorrow, are setting themselves up for failure. Best to begin with one liturgical Hour at a time. Add additional Hours gradually.

• **Look for natural spaces in your day.** Wondering which Hour(s) to pray? Determine where in your day it makes the most sense. If you tend to rise before the rest of the family to savor the quiet, then morning prayer is a natural for you. If you regularly find yourself sitting at an after-school sports practice or music lesson, evening prayer is an excellent way to use this time. Are lunch hours or breaks at work generally undisturbed? Daytime prayer for you.

• **Tie in prayer with a consistent event.** Just before breakfast. Just after dinner (while the children clear the table and do the dishes). While riding mass transit to work. Just before a favorite TV show. Just after a workout. Find the thing that always happens, and let prayer ride on its coattails.

• **Create your own monastery bells** in the form of cell phone alarms, pop-up reminders on your online calendar, oven timers, sticky notes, or just leaving your breviary, open to the next Hour, lying where you will see it.

• **Try podcasts while driving.** Listening to a podcast might be more an act of devotion than an act of liturgy—but for some people, it is at least a way to experience the daily psalms and unite one's intentions to the prayer of the Church. Commuters find the podcasts of divineoffice.org to be a godsend if they are not able to carve out time for prayer at home or at work.

• **Worth doing badly.** Consistency is important in keeping a habit going. Don't let the perfect be the enemy of the good. Don't even let the good be the enemy of the just barely okay. Suppose you generally find time to pray an Hour with time to reflect and hear what the Scriptures are telling you. But sometimes, life gets in the way and the twelve minutes you budgeted for morning prayer have evaporated to five. Or you are so distracted or upset that you can't possibly concentrate on the prayers. Certainly there's nothing wrong with skipping it. But skip it too often, and you might find that your habit is lost. My own experience of losing good habits all too quickly makes me follow G.K. Chesterton's maxim: A thing really worth doing is worth doing even badly. So when time has gotten away from me, I'll zoom through evening prayer in just a couple minutes rather than leave it out altogether. This is not the ideal for liturgical prayer, but for me it's the ideal way to maintain the habit. There will always be another day to pray with more thought and attention.

• **Learn to discern.** On the other hand, we have to acknowledge that our lives change. There are seasons of more activity or less, greater or fewer demands on our time. Your daily routine of liturgical prayer might run like a well-oiled machine for months, and then suddenly, bang! The baby is born. You are promoted at work to a position of huge responsibility. You have to go back to full-time work after years of working part-time. An aged parent needs your care. Know when it is time to scale back on the Liturgy of the Hours, without guilt, when your vocation appears to require it. You can always increase it when your life changes again later on.

The Psalms as Poetry and Song

Most of us are not huge fans of poetry. Even those who enjoyed studying it during high school and college may not be very likely to keep Keats, Frost, or Eliot on the nightstand along with the latest spy thrillers or those well-worn Jane Austen novels. Chalk it up to the decline in the culture—or the impatient modern personality that hasn't the time to ponder meter and metaphor. Unless you homeschool and poetry is in the kids' literature queue this year, iambs and trochees are probably not a huge portion of your literary diet.

On the other hand, we all like songs—jazz, pop tunes, Broadway stuff. We turn up the radio and sing along when a favorite comes on. We post on Facebook lines of song lyrics that strike us as funny, nostalgic, or in any way meaningful. This shows that we do have some patience for verbal finery after all—because those song lyrics are poetry. I'm not here to argue the merits of Shakespeare vs. Bono. My point is that we do like poetry that has been taught to us painlessly through aural repetition and the addition of music, which helps us feel the rhythm that is inherent in the words.

You know what I'm going to say next. The Psalms are poetry—lyrics of songs, to be precise. A particular type of poetry that remains poetry no matter what language it is translated into. Here's why:

• Being poetry, the Psalms speak to every condition of the human heart: joy, anger, despair, grief, exaltation, hope, love. And all these in relation to God.

• The Psalms use a poetic device that works no matter what the translation. It's called *parallelism*. That means (in extremely non-scholarly terms) that the poem says something, and then says it again in a different way for emphasis. Here are a few random psalm verses that use this device. Notice how in each case, the second line "parallels" the first.

From Psalm 88:

> For my soul is filled with evils;
> my life is on the brink of the grave.
> I am reckoned as one in the tomb;
> I have reached the end of my strength
> Why do you reject me, O Lord?
> Why do you hide your face?

From Psalm 67:

O God, be gracious and bless us
and let the light of your face shed its light upon us.
So will your ways be known upon earth
and all nations learn your salvation.

Not every psalm uses parallelism consistently, but many of them do. Noticing it will heighten your enjoyment of the Psalms. You will appreciate them as poems, even if you weren't an English major.

An Additional Note on Singing

Back in chapter five, we asked the question, "To sing or not to sing?" Let me expand my recommendation here, for the singing of the hymns and psalms can be a dynamic way to enrich your experience of the Liturgy of the Hours.

Much as we love to belt out a song in the shower, Catholics have a reputation of being shy liturgical singers. There's even a book about this phenomenon titled *Why Catholics Can't Sing*.[14] Arguing the whys and wherefores of this situation is not the topic here. Whether it's a matter of *can't*, or *won't*, the fact is that many of us *don't*. And that's too bad. Beyond questions of what kind of sacred music is more or less "singable" or more or less tasteful, many Catholics are simply too self-conscious to sing anything. And perhaps they've lost the concept of song as prayer.

In the General Instruction, the Church reminds us repeatedly that the Psalms were written as *songs*, not prose, and that song or chant is not really a decorative flourish that religious orders tack on to the Liturgy of the Hours. Rather, singing or chanting enhances or brings out the character of the liturgy to the highest degree.

Therefore, the Church strongly suggests that if you pray the Liturgy of the Hours *with a group*—such as a third order, a prayer group, or after weekday Mass with those who remain for it—that you consider singing at least some parts of it. This might be no more than the hymn at the beginning of the hour, the responsory after the reading, and the Our Father. Or perhaps, if someone in the group has a slight knowledge of music, it might be that learning and then teaching others some simple chants for the psalms should be explored. Singing part of the Liturgy of the Hours is especially recommended for Sundays, solemnities, and feasts.

If you are that slightly musical person in your group, you might wish to begin by teaching yourself some psalm tones using the *Mundelein Psalter* and its supporting website (see chapter three). Chant the hours at home yourself for a while until you have it down, and then arrange a teaching session with your group. It helps to have everyone "point" or mark the words of the psalms in their breviaries so that they know where to change from one note to the other. Perhaps the place to start this would be with the Gospel canticle, since this one marked page will be used whenever the group meets. Once the group is proficient at chanting the Gospel canticle, you can move on to learning to chant the psalms, if the enthusiasm is there. If not, well, at least you tried. But chances are that a group that has learned some simple chant will fall in love with both the contemplative rhythm and the sense of solemnity that it brings.

By now you know far more about the Liturgy of the Hours than most Catholics do. Even so, there are many more aspects to this beautiful way of prayer that could not be fully discussed in a book of this size. (For instance, a whole chapter could have been devoted to the ecumenical value of the Liturgy of the Hours.) Right now, you have more than enough information to successfully integrate the Liturgy of the Hours into your life. All that is left is to do it! If you haven't started yet, please start now, before the interest that inspired you to read this book wears off.

Pick up that breviary, or turn on that computer or mobile device. Find today's prayers, and choose the Hour you think yourself most likely to manage consistently. Mark your day planner, set up an alert on your computer, use the oven timer, or just put up a sticky note that says, "Evening Prayer after dinner" or "Night Prayer 9 PM." For the first few days, try to do this in a quiet place, away from the television and noisy children. You might use your bedroom, the backyard, the laundry room, or even the bathroom. Make yourself comfortable, open your breviary, and just begin. Take your time. It might help if you pray the words aloud or while silently moving your lips. This will slow you down, keep you focused, and keep both body and mind engaged in prayer.

Don't worry at first about doing everything exactly right. Just pray! As you become accustomed to the rhythm and pattern of antiphons, psalms, canticles, readings, and intercessions, things will fall into place. Any time you have questions, go for help! That might mean looking something up in this book, asking your pastor, or going to an online forum such as Catholic Answers. You may also write me anytime on my blog or through Franciscan Media. But while you wait to find the answer to your question, keep on praying your chosen Hour(s) faithfully. In the beginning, establishing a firm habit is more important than doing everything exactly right. Even if you use the wrong prayers for the day, leave out something, or get interrupted and don't finish the Hour, you are still praying the psalms and Scriptures. That in itself is an excellent devotion, one that will help you grow in knowledge of God's Word in faith, and in love.

The goal, of course, is to do even more than this. It is to become one in heart and mind with fellow Christians throughout the world, even throughout history, each time we step into that never-ceasing symphony of praise that ascends to heaven. You might think your own voice is a pathetic squeak compared to that of holy men and women consecrated to lives of prayer in hidden monasteries. But, in reality, you will add a unique and beautiful note to the eternal melody, and Our Lord—Jesus Christ himself—will sing it with you.

Thanks be to God.

1. General Instruction on the Liturgy of the Hours, 10–11.
2. General Audience, November 16, 2011.
3. See Apostolic Constitution on the Divine Office. 1–5; General Instruction on the Liturgy of the Hours, 218.
4. See *CCC*, 1546–1547.
5. Code of Canon Law, 1147.
6. *CCC*, 1174–1175.
7. General Audience, Wednesday, June 22, 2011. Available at http://www.vatican.va/holy_father/benedict_xvi/audiences/2011/documents/hf_benxvi_aud_20110622_en.html.
8. General Instruction for the Liturgy of the Hours, 15.
9. Translated by J.E. Tweed. From *Nicene and Post-Nicene Fathers, First Series*, Vol. 8. Edited by Philip Schaff. (Buffalo, N.Y.: Christian Literature, 1888.) Revised and edited for *New Advent* by Kevin Knight. http://www.newadvent.org/fathers/1801086.htm.
10. John Brook, *The School of Prayer*, (Liturgical), p. 5.
11. With Option B, the response "Lord, hear our prayer" is not used by anyone. The second half of the petition has become the response.
12. This example is not a precise quote from the Liturgy of the Hours, but rather a composite of a typical intercession.
13. C.S. Lewis, *Reflections on the Psalms* (New York: Harcourt Brace Jovanovich, 1958), p. 97.
14. Thomas Day, *Why Catholics Can't Sing: The Culture of Catholicism and the Triumph of Bad Taste* (New York: Crossroad, 1992).